EASY ECONOMICS

EASY ECONOMICS

A Visual Guide to What You Need to Know

BY LEONARD WOLFE WITH LEE SMITH AND STEPHEN BUCKLES

Illustrations by Roy Doty

WILEY

John Wiley & Sons, Inc.

Copyright © 2012 by Leonard Wolfe. All rights reserved.

Published by John Wiley & Sons, Inc., Hoboken, New Jersey.

Published simultaneously in Canada.

For general information on our other products and services or for technical support, please contact our Customer Care Department within the United States at (800) 762-2974, outside the United States at (317) 572-3993 or fax (317) 572-4002.

Wiley publishes in a variety of print and electronic formats and by print-on-demand. Some material included with standard print versions of this book may not be included in e-books or in print-on-demand. If this book refers to media such as a CD or DVD that is not included in the version you purchased, you may download this material at http://booksupport.wiley.com. For more information about Wiley products, visit www.wiley.com.

ISBN: 978-1-118-11806-1 (pbk); ISBN 978-1-118-21899-0 (ebk); ISBN 978-1-118-21900-3 (ebk); ISBN 978-1-118-21901-0 (ebk)

Printed in the United States of America

10 9 8 7 6 5 4 3 2 1

WHAT THIS BOOK IS ABOUT

Given that you were drawn to this book, chances are you are bright, educated, and intellectually curious. And like most bright, educated people you probably know very little about economics.

Unfortunately, few of us have much of a grip on economics, even when we are well-informed on other matters. But economic literacy is vital to making sense of the world we live in. We have witnessed bewildering turmoil in the economy and the deepest economic decline since the 1930s. We have been introduced to gobbledygook terms like collateralized debt obligations and credit default swaps. We have been confounded by subprime mortgage defaults, too-big-to-fail financial institutions, toxic assets, and economic collapse in countries we never paid much attention to before. A "haircut" is no longer just something you get at the barbershop, but also a loss on a bad loan.

This book aims to bring you up to speed, in a way that entertains while it informs. Don't let the cartoons fool you into thinking this book is frivolous. The information is solid. We've collected many of the most frequently asked questions—plus some you haven't thought of—on the subject of economics. Our topics range from the beginnings of money, to what makes economies grow, to whether Social Security will survive, to the benefits and costs of globalization. No question, in our view, is too dumb to ask and no answer should be too hard to understand. We've tried to provide answers that are as untechnical and jargon-free as possible without shortchanging you or insulting your intelligence.

Reading this book won't make you a candidate for a Nobel Prize, but it will make you more comfortable with many of the ideas that underlie today's important economic issues.

Lee Smith served as a senior writer and member of the Board of Editors of *Fortune* for 20 years and was its Bureau Chief both in Washington and in Tokyo, where his articles won citations for excellence from the Overseas Press Club of America. Prior to *Fortune*, he was a state capital correspondent for the Associated Press and a staff writer for *Newsweek*. Other publications for which he has written include *Time* and *U.S. News & World Report*.

Roy Doty is an internationally renowned illustrator whose work has appeared in the *New York Times*, *Fortune*, *Newsweek*, *BusinessWeek*, *Sports Illustrated*, and *Golf Digest*. He has written or co-authored 29 books, illustrated more than 160, and produced advertising and promotional work for many corporations in the United States and abroad. He has been named "Illustrator of the Year" six times by the National Cartoonist Society, and at its 2011 annual convention he received the Gold Key award and was inducted into the Cartoon Hall of Fame, becoming only the 13th member to be so honored in 65 years.

Leonard Wolfe spent more than 20 years at Time Inc. as an art director. He designed many of Time-Life Books' most successful series, was Associate Art Director of *Fortune*, founding art director of Time Inc.'s science magazine *Discover*, and Promotion Art Director of *Time* magazine. Following his career at Time Inc., he founded a corporate communications company that produced annual reports and corporate literature for Perrier, GE, Time Warner, ExxonMobil, *Reader's Digest*, *BusinessWeek*, and the *Wall Street Journal*, among many others.

Richard Warner has led a distinguished career as an art director and educator. He was Art Director of *Sports Illustrated* following his early years as a professor of design at Southern Methodist University. Most recently, he has been involved in corporate design, producing editorial and promotion materials for GE, ExxonMobil, Time Inc., GM, and BestFoods.

Stephen Buckles has enjoyed a distinguished career as a university professor, author, and leader of many respected professional organizations. A specialist in economics education, he has received numerous awards for his contributions to that field. He has been a board member of the Journal of Economics Education, economics editor of the *Business Journal*, President of the National Council on Economic Education, and Chair of the Individual Investors Advisory Committee of the New York Stock Exchange. He currently teaches economics at Vanderbilt University.

Barry Meinerth served as a Senior Vice President at Time Inc., responsible for printing and fulfillment of the company's books and magazines throughout the world. Prior to that, he was Business Manager of both *Time International* and *Discover* magazines, Circulation Director of *Time International*, and Production Director of *Fortune*.

ACKNOWLEDGMENTS

Creating this book has been both a pleasure and an education in it-self. And like any other worthwhile project, it has required the skill, talent, and experience of a number of dedicated individuals who saw the book's promise from the very beginning and were willing to de-vote many hours to making it the informative, inviting, and enter-taining book it has become.

It began with a core staff of former colleagues from Time Inc. and soon grew to include other accomplished members with equally im-pressive backgrounds. Together they brought a combined wealth of experience, knowledge, and talent to create a unique view of a subject that for many has often seemed a formidable and intimidating one.

Credit belongs to a long list of people, but foremost among them are Roy Doty, Lee Smith, Stephen Buckles, and Richard Warner.

Roy has always managed to take complicated issues and ideas, condense their messages, and present them in a charming and delightful way, and he has done so here with cartoons that both inform and entertain.

Lee's ability to write clearly, concisely, and with an easygoing style makes even the most arcane subject matter come alive in the most interesting way imaginable.

Steve's impressive background in economics education has proven invaluable, and the wealth of knowledge that he has brought to the book makes it one whose substance and content one can count on with confidence.

Richard's elegant format design sets the stage for the beautiful visual presentation that is apparent with each turn of the page.

Thanks, too, to Barry Meinerth, whose business acumen has been invaluable. To Marisa Gentile Raffio, whose unruffled professional manner under sometimes trying conditions made the production of the book far easier than it might have been and who has been a pleas-ure to work with. And to Ruth Wolfe, whose talent and experience in copyediting and proofreading played an important part in assuring the book's conciseness and clarity.

Special thanks, too, to Caroline Gallagher Donnelly, who was involved in the book's early planning and development. And addi-tional thanks to former colleagues at *Fortune*, William Rukeyser and Al Ehrbar, as well as to Michele Kalishman, Socrates Nicholas, Greg Rogers, Steve Rogers, and others too many to mention here.

To all of you, thanks for an exceptional job well done.

Leonard Wolfe

CONTENTS

EASY **ECONOMICS**

chapter 1
Money

*It's fairy dust, but because
we believe in it, it works*

INTRODUCTION

Money sometimes seems to be what economics is all about. It's what we work to get and what we pay out to survive. It's what makes the world go around, pretty much the way Joel Grey sings it in his cynical, yet joyful number in the musical *Cabaret*. But look at it again. You can't eat it, drive it, or wear it. Stripped of its mystique, money is just a convenient way of exchanging goods and services, big or small, banal or exotic. Today's paper money and electronic money exist only because we believe in them. To make another theatrical allusion, money is like *Peter Pan*'s Tinker Bell, who is kept alive only because the audience believes in her. We believe in money— oh, yes we do. We believe that crumpled piece of paper with $5 on it can actually be exchanged for something to eat. Even more remarkably, we accept the fact that after a hard week's work, we are going to be paid with nothing but a bunch of electrons sent to the bank. Money is based on faith, but because all of us, or almost all of us, keep the faith, money works. How did we get this way?

What happened before there was money?

In early societies where people lived by hunting and gathering, they probably shared goods and services without any immediate payback. The hunters who dragged home a water buffalo didn't demand a load of firewood right away. They knew the family or tribe would keep them warm. But barter certainly came into practice early on, especially as villages got larger and people had to deal with those who weren't family. Through most of history, barter has been a simple and obvious way of trading goods, even with strangers, almost as natural as language. Five-year-old children without instructions from their parents know how to trade a toy truck for a toy train. As they get older, children can make sophisticated judgments about markets. "I know from what I've seen that around here, one Derek Jeter baseball card is worth two Albert Pujols," one eight-year-old can confidently tell another.

Q&A

When did barter become popular?

A

The history of bartering as a widespread practice goes back to 6000 B.C. in the Middle East, among the tribes in what was then Mesopotamia. The practice spread to the Phoenicians, who lived along the Mediterranean coast in what is today Lebanon and Syria. Beginning about 1200 B.C., the Phoenicians became the Mediterranean's great traders, carrying wine, cedar logs, perfumes, dyes, and spices among ports from Egypt to the Iberian peninsula. Barter worked just about anywhere, in local trade as well as international. European swineherds could successfully trade pigs for wheat; cattlemen could swap for horses. Salt was so valuable in the Roman Empire that soldiers would accept it as barter for their military service.

Isn't barter an awkward way to trade?

It certainly has its limitations. Perhaps you had a horse that you were eager to trade for a cow. But the owner of the cow didn't want a horse; he wanted wheat. So you had to hunt down a wheat farmer who needed a horse. You traded with him and took the wheat to the cow owner, who was then satisfied. That was time consuming. Also, you might be able to trade off one horse that way, but suppose that you had a team of horses that you wanted to get rid of and there were no immediate buyers.

How did traders get around that complication?

One way was to use storehouses. If a farmer had more livestock and grain on hand than he could pass along immediately, he could give it to the keeper of a storehouse. The keeper would hand him receipts, and he could later present the receipts and get his livestock and grain back. Or, he could give those receipts to someone else in exchange for, say, a house or a team of horses or whatever. And that was one of the beginnings of money. A piece of paper, in this case a warehouse receipt, could be used in exchange for something of real value, a house. That was one of the origins of money.

When did coins appear?

Money did not evolve over the centuries from a single source. Warehouse receipts were one line of development. Coins made from precious metals like gold and silver were another. Pieces of copper that may have been coins were found in a tomb in China dating from the 11th century B.C. Both warehouse receipts and precious metals are more convenient to carry around for trading than horses and pigs. But in other respects these two forms of money are quite different. As paper or parchment, warehouse receipts themselves have little value. Silver and gold, on the other hand, have at least some intrinsic value. Silver can be turned into bracelets and goblets. Gold has always had bling, universally and almost mystically revered as a demonstration of beauty and power. (Many investors, so-called "gold bugs," still think it's the surest way to store one's wealth.) About the year 600 B.C., Athenians, who had a plentiful supply of silver, began to press coins of high quality and uniform silver content. Athenian traders and later Alexander the Great spread the coins throughout the Greek world. The Athenian "owl" (the coin had a portrait of Athena on one side and an owl on the other) became a standard currency of the ancient world, much as the dollar is today.

Who decides what money is?

Over the centuries, it has generally been markets, not governments, that ultimately have decided what money is. Things that a lot of people want, that are relatively scarce and are portable, have been used as currency. "Liquidity" is an important attribute. Your Lamborghini is valuable, but it would make a poor currency because you probably can't sell it in a hurry for a top price and you can't easily break off parts of it for sale. Investors measure the value of their holdings partly in terms of liquidity, asking how many of those stock certificates, bonds, real estate investments, condo time shares, antique chairs, and 1930s comic books can quickly be turned into cash, which generally means dollars or another international currency. Over the centuries unusual

forms of currency have come and gone. The Lenape Indians apparently accepted axes, hoes, cauldrons, awls, and wampum beads in exchange for Manhattan Island. (The historical record is a little shaky on this trade, but the value seems to have been about $24 then, roughly $1,000 now.) A serious shortage of coins throughout the British Empire in the late 1700s led to the development of an unusual currency, one that was literally liquid, in the colony of New South Wales, Australia. Highly sought after, storable, transportable, and easily divisible into portions, imported rum became the most accepted currency in the land. In the Moscow of the 1980s, cab drivers much preferred to be paid in Marlboro cigarettes than in rubles.

When did paper money begin?

We mentioned warehouse receipts for cattle and grain a little earlier. But in 17th century England a much broader and more significant form of paper money began to emerge. Merchants and traders had amassed huge hoards of gold and put it in the Royal Mint for storage. But in 1640, King Charles I seized the gold to fund his troops in the English Civil War. Understandably, the seizure made the merchants nervous, so they decided to save their future gold in the private vaults of London goldsmiths, whom they paid a fee for the privilege. The goldsmith gave the merchant a receipt certifying the quantity and purity of his gold, and when the merchant wanted his gold back he could present the merchant his receipt.

Or the merchant could use his stock of gold to create, in effect, his own paper money. Let's suppose a fabric manufacturer who has gold stored with the goldsmith needs sheep's wool. He can hand an order that says "pay the bearer of this certificate three ounces of gold" to the shepherd, who then turns the order over to a merchant in exchange for bags of wheat. The order keeps changing hands in a long train of purchases until some recipient, the swineherd perhaps, turns it over to the goldsmith for three ounces of gold. The goldsmiths of 17th century London were the forerunners of today's British bankers.

Q&A

What did early Americans use for money?

Colonial Americans used all kinds of things, including furs, tobacco, Indian wampum, and Spanish and Portuguese coins. The Massachusetts Bay Colony created the first banknotes on American soil in 1690, when the colonial government in Boston, short of gold and coins, paid soldiers with paper that could be later exchanged for gold or silver coins. Maybe Boston could and maybe it couldn't make good on all that paper, but the promise won the citizens' confidence, and the notes stayed in circulation and were considered money. Other colonies, also short of coins, copied Massachusetts. During the Revolution, the Continental Congress paid war expenses in paper money called Continentals—so many of them to so many soldiers and to so many suppliers, with little valuable metal to back them up, that by the end of the war Continentals were worthless. Twice in the early years of the U.S., the federal government tried to support national banks that would issue a stable currency accepted and recognized by all Americans. After the second bank failed in 1837, commercial banks around the country continued to issue their own notes, in such proliferation that at one time there were 5,000 different kinds of banknotes in circulation. That was bewildering. If you received a banknote with the name of a big, creditworthy bank on it, the note might be good countrywide. But many notes had no value farther than a few miles from home.

How did we get to the dollar bill?

During the opening year of the Civil War, 1861, the Union army ran gigantic expenses, far beyond the ability of the government to pay out of its meager tax receipts. So, Congress authorized President Lincoln's government to issue $50 million worth of Treasury notes to pay soldiers and arms suppliers and the rest. Early on, those notes were supposedly exchangeable for silver or gold. But it soon became obvious there was no way Washington could turn all of those notes into precious metals. So in 1862, President Lincoln's aides created a new note, the "green-back," in denominations of $5, $10, $20, and up, with an appearance not remarkably different from today's dollar bills. Greenbacks were significantly different from the 1861 notes. These earlier notes promised they were convertible into coins. The greenback simply said "This note is a legal tender." It was "fiat" money—money because the government said it was money. It worked. People accepted greenbacks, even though the government would not exchange them for precious metals. The fact that the Union won the war almost certainly had a bearing on that.

Q&A

If it isn't backed by gold, what makes the dollar mighty?

Up until 1971, the dollar was backed by gold, sort of. Neither American nor foreign citizens could exchange their dollars for gold. But foreign governments could convert some of the dollars they held at the set rate of $35 an ounce, the gold standard. President Nixon ended that practice because foreign governments, nervous about the U.S. economy, began to convert their dollars into gold in large volumes, running down American gold reserves. Taken off the gold standard, the dollar lost its supreme value, as any American tourist traveling in Europe after 1971 can attest. (It was good news for U.S. manufacturers, however, because it made their products cheaper for foreigners to buy.) Today the dollar's international value depends on the familiar tug between supply and demand. We discuss this in greater detail in Chapter 7, but basically it means that foreigners create a demand for dollars because they want to buy Johnson & Johnson heart devices or trips to the Grand Canyon or, more likely, U.S. stocks and bonds. Moreover, they want to hold their money in dollars because the U.S. economy and political system still guarantee that it is the most secure place on earth. The dollar, although it fluctuates daily and sometimes greatly in value relative to other currencies, still projects power. If you pull your tanker up to an oil spigot in the Persian Gulf, for example, the price is calculated in dollars, not euros, pesos, or yen.

Q&A

When did checking accounts start?

Accepting a check requires an even greater leap of faith than accepting paper currency not backed by gold or silver. A ten-year-old can understand why a $10 bill can be translated into a movie ticket and candy. But how does his father get away with writing any amount of money he wants on a blank piece of paper and trading it to a car dealer for four wheels? The first widely used checks were probably those introduced in the 1500s in Holland. Amsterdam was then a major international shipping and trading center. People who had accumulated cash began depositing it with Dutch "cashiers," for a fee, as a safer alternative to keeping the money at home. Eventually the cashiers agreed to pay their depositors' debts out of the money in each account, based on the depositor's written order to do so. Before World War II, U.S. workers were commonly paid in cash and settled their bills the same way, putting anything left over into savings accounts. In the 1950s, checking accounts got a foothold in the middle class, climbed rapidly in acceptance, and may have peaked in the mid-1990s when Americans wrote 50 billion checks a year. Most checks are good, but those Americans who unwittingly accept bad checks typically are defrauded out of $1 billion or so annually. The puzzled 10-year-old skeptic has a point.

Q&A

Why did electronic money catch on?

Even though there are currently about $32 trillion worth of checks written every year in the U.S. alone, the use of checks to transfer funds is probably in decline, losing out to electronic transactions. Financial institutions, for example, no longer write millions of dollars of checks to one another to settle accounts. It is much faster and cheaper to send money back and forth by electronic signals. In a typical year, banks and other financial institutions move around a staggering $40 trillion or more worth of electrons. Consumers, too, are converting from heavy reliance on checking accounts to more use of electrons through credit cards and online banking. Their reasoning is clear: It is simply easier.

Q&A

Will paper money disappear?

Paper money in day-to-day circulation now accounts for only 10% of the U.S.'s total money supply of roughly $9 trillion. The other 90% is in deposits in many different kinds of accounts, from simple savings and checking accounts to complex money market funds and sophisticated certificates of deposit. Surprisingly, a huge but uncertain number of those dollar bills in various denominations circulate outside the U.S. Economists guess that dollars abroad amount to about $600 billion of the total $900 billion in circulation. What are they doing out there? Yes, some are engaged in the drug trade and other illegal pursuits. But in other places, such as Panama, El Salvador, and Ecuador, the dollar is the official currency. And in many other places people want to have dollars in their drawers or safe deposit boxes because dollars are sound and accepted pretty much everywhere. If you have to leave the country in a hurry, dollars will ease your travel. Within the U.S., however, paper currency may be in decline, losing out to electrons in the same way checks are losing out. It will become increasingly simple to run your cell phone over the bar code on the packages at the supermarket and have your cereal boxes and paper towels charged directly to your credit card account. No need to wait in line for the cashier. How long will it be before you can scan everything into your cell phone?

Q&A

Q

Whatever happened to barter?

A

Barter, as we all know, has never disappeared. Neighbors, friends, and others still trade goods and services without money changing hands. "If you pave my patio," the auto mechanic tells the mason, "You can take my old Chevy." No-money transactions can be challenging for the IRS, because they are officially taxable but not always reported as income, and they are hard to detect. Interestingly, the Internet, the very modern communications system, has invigorated barter, the most ancient of exchange systems. There is now a universe of online websites on which consumers trade everything from umbrella stands to second homes. Businesses, too, barter more than they used to because the Internet has made such shopping reasonably efficient. (Businesses presumably pay taxes.) The International Reciprocal Trade Association, a global trade association for the barter industry, estimates that 400,000 businesses around the world barter and that their transactions amounted to about $12 billion in 2010. That's peanuts, of course, a fraction of total world trade, which amounted to about $12 trillion that year. Still, Internet barter has made possible some dizzying exchanges that would have been impossible otherwise. Consider the nation in Latin America that had excess aircraft. A sister Latin American nation wanted the aircraft but had only bananas to offer in exchange. The aircraft owner didn't care for bananas; it wanted earthmovers. So the banana producer began an around-the-world trek by Internet. It traded bananas for oil in the Middle East, then oil for warehouses of rugs in South Asia, which were transferred to Japan for earthmovers. The Latin American nation that had started out with bananas finally had the earthmovers the aircraft owner desired. Trade accomplished. Barter lives.

chapter 2
Booms & Busts

*As smart as they are, the pros can't remove
all the bone-rattling bumps*

INTRODUCTION

Both words in this chapter title discomfort governments, busts for obvious reasons. Booms can be disquieting, too. Countries emerging from centuries of rural poverty, like China and India, can grow at a rate of 9% or 10% a year for some time without imploding. But a mature economy like that of the U.S. would soon overheat and boil with inflation. Better for the U.S. to grow steadily year after year at a rate of 3% or 4%. Unfortunately, economies are not so well behaved. Growth over time is marked by booms and busts. Since its beginning as a nation, the U.S. has suffered through almost 50 recessions. The biggest downturn in recent times was the Great Depression of the 1930s, during which the gross domestic product (GDP) dropped by an astounding 27%. The economy boomed after World War II and then quieted down with only relatively small setbacks. Economists in the Kennedy Administration were convinced they could fine-tune the economy, eliminate the ups and downs by tweaking fiscal and monetary policy. The tools weren't completely successful, but the several recessions that followed were relatively mild. Later, the years from 1983 to 2007 are called by economists the Great Moderation, a period of fewer and more gentle ups and downs. Then calamity struck, beginning with a collapse in the housing market in late 2007, followed by the greatest general economic tumble since the 1930s. It became known as the Great Recession. What causes the sickening roller-coaster rides of booms and busts? Can they be prevented?

What do the experts mean when they say the economy
is doing well or is doing poorly?

Generally they are referring to the growth—or shrinkage—of the gross
domestic product, the GDP, which means the nation's total output of goods
and services; increases or decreases in the inflation rate; changes in the
unemployment rate; and the growth of workplace productivity, or lack of it.

Q&A

Q *What makes up the GDP?*

A

It is broken into four major parts: **Consumer spending,** the most important factor by far, accounts for about two-thirds. That's why the experts pay so much attention to consumer spending on everything from airplane tickets to cars to yoga classes as an indicator of where the economy is headed. **Government spending,** the second part, accounts for a little less than 20%; the category includes everything from the salaries of soldiers and their weapons and technicians at the Centers for Disease Control, which are federal expenses, to the salaries of school teachers and road repair, generally state and local undertakings. The third part is **business investment,** which usually accounts for 15% or more. This category doesn't refer to business spending, as when Apple buys glass for its iPads or Ford buys steel to make F-150 pickup trucks. (That spending doesn't get counted as part of GDP until consumers buy iPads and F-150s.) Business investment is when Ford retools an old factory to build an electric car, or Apple spends money to develop the iNextgadget. The investment category also includes the amount of money people spend on new houses and all the fittings that come with them. But it does not include the sale of existing homes, because nothing new has been produced. The fourth part is **export spending,** which consists of all the goods and services— airplanes, food, software, and the rest—that are produced here and sold abroad. That would add another 10–13% to GDP, but you have to subtract an amount equivalent to all that we import—all the autos, toys, wine, and a long list of other products and services made outside the U.S. but consumed here. Imports come to the equivalent of 14–18% of GDP.

What makes the GDP grow?

It comes down to two words: demand and supply. Consumers demand—and buy—more cell phones and strollers; government buys more computers, hires more park rangers, recruits more Marines; energy companies build windmills; Japan buys more Nebraska wheat. GDP also depends upon supply, our abilities to produce goods and services. How much labor, how skilled is that labor, how many machines, tools, factories, and office buildings do we have, and how much technology are we able to use? All influence how much we are able to produce.

When is the economy booming?

A growth rate in the GDP of 3% or better is good. About 1% of that growth would be the additional incomes of the 1.5 million immigrants and young people coming out of high school and college, who join the 150 million-plus U.S. labor force each year. (The other 2% would come from increases in productivity, which we will explain shortly.) Employment will never be, and should never be, 100%, because at all times some of the 150 million-plus will be changing jobs and therefore are not counted. Also, do you have a brother-in-law who is really incompetent and unable to hold onto a job in normal times? When that brother-in-law manages to stay in a job for a while it could be a sign that the economy is growing too fast; in its overheated condition employers are hiring anyone.

Why is overheating bad?

For one thing it leads to inflation. Imagine that everyone is employed, factories are running flat out, restaurants are jammed. Inefficient factories that had been closed are reopened, and incompetent, or at least inexperienced, employees are hired. The combination of outdated plants and inept employees can't keep up with demand. Spending is growing faster than production. Because everyone is employed and has cash, they bid up the prices of the limited number of cars, computers, restaurant meals, and everything else. That's inflation, or at least one form of inflation. Consumers and businesses alike are baffled and worried, finding it difficult to plan their budgets for the months ahead. People who can't easily bargain for higher wages, such as the retired and those locked in labor contracts, get angry.

Q&A

What's productivity?

That's a function of the economy that laymen don't pay much attention to, but one that the experts focus on. Growth in productivity means that there are more goods and services available to satisfy consumer demands without consumers having to battle one another. Go back to the inflation scenario of the previous question. Imagine that 10 autoworkers can produce no more than 20 cars in a 40-hour workweek. In a heated economy many eager buyers, flush with dollars, bid up the prices of those cars from, say, $20,000 to $25,000. When those numbers reach the national GDP count, it will look as though the economy has grown by the number of cars sold times $5,000. But that is only what is called "nominal" growth, representing nothing more than inflation. Consider those same 10 autoworkers again. Imagine that because they are professionals gaining experience and working with the latest equipment, they can now turn out 22 cars during that same 40-hour workweek. That's a jump in productivity of 10%, creating two more cars to satisfy consumer demand. Jack and Jill don't have to fight over a car; each can have one. This is real GDP growth, not just inflation.

Q

How does an overheated economy cool down?

A

Often the Federal Reserve cools it down by raising interest rates. It becomes more expensive for businesses and consumers to borrow money, so demand falls. Keep in mind that demand is not just what people want; it is what they have the money to buy. But if demand falls too far, the economy grinds to a halt.

Is that what causes a recession?

Yes, when demand keeps falling or does not rise as rapidly as production, the economy stumbles into recession. The definition of recession is a little vague, but basically it means a significant decline in activity spread across the economy and lasting for more than a few months. That lays a deadening hand on employment. Recall that just to absorb the crowd of new high school and college graduates and immigrants who burst into the labor market every year, the economy has to create 1.5 million new jobs.

What is deflation?

It's the opposite of inflation and means that prices are actually falling. That sounds great, at first. You can buy cells phones and disc players for next to nothing. Yippee! It is great when prices are going down because manufacturers have learned how to make their devices more cheaply, can lower prices, and still make a profit. But it is an enormous problem if manufacturers lower the prices simply to move the merchandise, even at a loss, or if hotel owners cut prices just to fill rooms. Consumers—and that includes businesses that are buying supplies and services from other businesses—will hesitate to buy, waiting for prices to fall still further. Eventually, manufacturers will close their factories and hotels will shut their rooms because the future looks so gloomy. The employees they fire will have less money to spend and even those who still have jobs will hold onto their money, anxious about their own employment and expecting prices to fall still further. Many experts consider the downward spiral of deflation even more menacing than inflation.

Q

How do you end a recession?

A

Some of those who have thought about the question would answer that you simply wait it out. The movement from hot to cold and back to hot is a natural phenomenon—the "business cycle"—and it is fruitless to interfere. But it is hard to look on indifferently when fellow citizens are suffering both economic and psychological pain as they wait for the cycle to turn enough to provide jobs.

There are two basic ways for the federal government to stimulate the economy. For one, the Federal Reserve can increase the money supply, putting more money in banks for people and businesses to borrow. (We'll discuss that in detail in Chapter 5.) The other way to speed the spin of the cycle is to create demand. But how to do that? Here, well-meaning cycle-spinners are divided. Liberals generally argue that the way to do it is to increase government spending on projects that will put people to work. Conservatives maintain that the best way to increase demand is to cut taxes and thereby put more money in the hands of businesses and consumers who will go out and spend it. Which side is right? Both. Government spending on highways, education, and other programs definitely creates jobs. When consumers get tax breaks, they are indeed more likely to replace their kitchen appliances or take longer vacations. Which method is more efficient, gets more money into the economy with more wallop? That's a question of endless debate that will not be entered into here.

Q&A

Q How long can a bust last?

A

The Great Depression lasted all the way through the 1930s, with unemployment rising to as high as 25% at times. World War II, and the colossal demand it created for guns, planes, ships, men for battle, and women for factories, decisively put an end to that bust. After the war, deprived consumers were starved for houses, cars, and all the rest. The economy boomed.

The Great Recession that began with the collapse of the housing market in 2007 proved to be surprisingly stubborn. Constructing houses not only puts to work carpenters, plumbers, electricians, and real estate agents. Houses have to be filled with refrigerators, air conditioners, carpets, blinds, windows, and much more. Think of the factories that turn out those appliances and fittings and the supply train needed to get them to construction sites. Four years after the collapse of the housing market, unemployment remained at 9%, almost twice what economists consider an acceptable rate for a healthy economy. Not since the Great Depression had the economy been so sluggish for so long. On average, post World War II recessions lasted no more than 11 months. (Some recessions, however, had been deeper, even though shorter; in the 1981–1982 recession, unemployment was stuck at more than 10% for 10 months.)

What forces could boost employment? Could government do it? The Federal Reserve was doing its best to guarantee an ample supply of money at low interest rates so that entrepreneurs could start new businesses and managers could expand established ones. Banks were urged to lend to consumers as well, so they could buy cars and houses and more. The Fed, in bringing interest rates essentially down to zero, had exhausted all of its traditional tools (see Chapter 5). The results were not dramatic, at least not immediately. But a strong case could be made that without the Fed's extraordinary efforts, the unemployment rate would have been higher still.

Would fiscal policy help (see Chapter 3)? First, the Bush and then the Obama administrations had tried multibillion-dollar stimulus programs on highways, water and sewer projects, education, increased unemployment and welfare benefits, and increased payments to state and local governments to stimulate the flagging economy. After those programs ran their courses, Washington seemed deadlocked on whether to continue using fiscal tools. Liberals wanted to spend more money on programs that would create jobs. Would that work? The billions that had already been spent on stimulus programs had not brought the unemployment rate below 9%. But, as with the actions by the Fed, it's likely that unemployment would have been significantly higher without those programs. Conservatives wanted to move in the opposite direction:

reduce spending to get the budget under control and reassure the business community that the country was stable and ready for investment. That was undoubtedly a good idea for later in the decade, but was of questionable value in meeting the immediate challenge of kicking the economy into gear.

Exports might have energized the U.S. economy, but Europeans were trying to cope with the burden of their governments' debts and were not feeling rich and eager to buy U.S. goods. Would countries with expanding economies like Brazil, China, and India encourage their businesses and consumers to spend their money on imports? The prospects were not encouraging.

Where would it end? Busts don't last forever. U.S. businesses, not counting financial firms, were sitting on almost $2 trillion in cash, ready to boost their offerings of goods and services and expand their work forces when consumers, who account for almost two-thirds of GDP, bucked up and started shopping again. Eventually consumers would regain their confidence and their appetites and resume spending. But history shows that can take a long time.

chapter 3
Taxing & Spending

Policy makers often argue over which
is a better steering wheel

INTRODUCTION

Government collects taxes to pay for its spending. That's simple enough and understandable. But taxing and spending—fiscal policy, as it is formally known—have other purposes as well. Government can use changes in spending and taxing to encourage behavior it considers a boon to society or discourage behavior it considers a bane. Because homeowners may have a greater interest and stake in the local community than renters, income spent on the interest share of mortgage payments is tax free; income spent on rent is not. A check you send to a shelter for battered women or a painting you give to a museum can also lower your tax bill. Money earned on the sale of stock or the sale of the family business—capital gains—is taxed at a lower rate than paycheck income in the belief that it persuades people to invest in businesses. Businesses create jobs and income. Conversely, "sin taxes," like the heavy ones on cigarettes, discourage behavior most of us disapprove of. Smoking burdens the health care system. And there is still another reason for changing taxes and spending. Fiscal policy can be used as a rudder to help steer the economy. (The other rudder is monetary policy, which we discuss in Chapter 5.) If the economy is sluggish, government can cut taxes and increase spending to energize it.

What is fiscal policy?

The federal government has two ways of making a direct impact on the economy. One is through increasing and decreasing the money supply, the responsibility of the Federal Reserve, as we'll talk about in Chapter 5. The other is fiscal policy, which is all about taxing and spending—and also about borrowing, because there is almost always a gap between how much the government brings in as taxes and how much it spends.

Q&A

Who controls tax policy?

A

Both Congress and the President. Let's start with taxing. The Constitution says that all tax bills have to begin in the House Ways & Means Committee. (The name goes back to the British Parliament and American colonial legislatures, and simply refers to "ways and means" of financing programs.) The chairman of the committee is the senior Republican on the committee when Republicans have control of the House and the senior Democrat when the Democrats are running things. The chairman automatically becomes one of the most powerful people in Congress. The committee comes up with a plan to raise some taxes, cut others; every now and then, it proposes to revise the entire tax code. The whole House approves the plan and passes it to the Senate. The Senate Finance Committee does not have the same Constitutional assignment as Ways and Means, but it clearly has great influence over what the Senate adds to and cuts out of tax legislation. When the House and Senate agree on tax legislation, they pass it down Pennsylvania Avenue to the White House. The real world, of course, is much more complex. The plan that reaches the White House does not take the President by surprise. Like hundreds of other interest groups, the White House has lobbyists who patrol Congressional office buildings constantly, urging Senators and Congressmen and women to reduce one tax or pump up another.

Where do taxes come from?

Overwhelmingly, federal taxes come from individual taxpayers: about 45% from income taxes and 35% from Social Security and Medicare taxes, sometimes known as payroll taxes. Another 12% or so of total tax receipts comes from corporate income taxes. Much of the rest is excise taxes on everything from gasoline, alcohol, and cigarettes to planes and fishing equipment. Early on in U.S. history most taxes came from

tariffs collected on imported goods, which was why the predecessor of the Coast Guard (the Revenue Cutter Service) was part of the Treasury Department; its job was to foil smugglers. Another big source of revenue was taxes on whiskey, much resented by many distillers. President George Washington, a distiller himself and compliant taxpayer, led troops against refusnik whiskey makers in Pennsylvania.

How come the rich get away without paying taxes?

That's a misconception. The rich pay a lot. The top 5% of income earners in the U.S. pay almost 45 % of all federal income taxes. At the other end, almost half of American workers, those in relatively low income brackets, pay no income taxes at all, although they do pay hefty Social Security and Medicare taxes. But there's a moral argument that the rich should pay even more than they already do. If you need more tax revenues, an extra dollar in taxes is much less painful for a rich man than for an average one. The U.S. has a graduated, progressive tax code. That means that those who earn the most not only pay the most, but pay at a higher rate. If your income is $75,000, you likely pay $15,000 or so in income taxes, or 20% of your income. If your income is $75 million, you might be taxed at a rate of 35%, which would bring your tax bill to a little over $26 million. However, the wealthy can hire legions of accountants and lawyers to find ways to make their tax bills as small as possible. For example, ordinary income of the kind that comes in a paycheck is taxed at 35%. But capital gains income, such as the kind that comes from the sale of stock or the $1 million profit on the sale of a beach home or ski lodge, is taxed at lower rates. So the more income that can be moved around and labeled capital gains, the better. That's just one of the ways the wealthy can lower their tax bills.

What's a flat tax?

A

In its purest form it's a tax in which everybody, rich or average (the poor don't pay income taxes) would be taxed at the same rate. The first $20,000 or $30,000 of everybody's income would be tax free in most proposals for a flat tax. After that everybody's income would be taxed at a rate of, say, 25%. There would be no deductions for expenses like interest payments on home mortgages or the many other loopholes in the tax code. Proponents point out that a flat tax would eliminate the finagling and shady accounting and lost revenues for the government that accompany the complexity of the current tax code; the change would also save taxpayers multimillions of dollars in tax advice. Losers would include not only lawyers and accountants but also charities that count on tax-deductible contributions. The housing industry would be perplexed, at least for a while, by the elimination of the mortgage interest deduction for homeowners. (Interestingly, despite the housing industry's determination to retain that deduction, only about one-quarter of homeowners actually claim it on their tax returns.) If a flat tax were enacted, average folks might wind up paying more taxes and rich folks less. Nonetheless, the idea seems to have a surprising amount of support from average taxpayers, perhaps because they believe the rich now pay no taxes at all. Some of the rich get away with paying little or no taxes, but, as noted previously, most of them pay a lot of taxes.

Q&A

Q What's a consumption tax?

A

Basically it's a sales tax, familiar to most of us because a majority of states and many cities levy sales taxes on many items, although they generally exempt things like food and medicine. Some economists and others think the federal government should levy a sales or consumption tax as well and reduce income taxes by a comparable amount of money. The argument for doing so is that it would increase the amount of money that people save. Why? Because money you save would not be taxed, at least not until much later when you spend it. This would be good for us as individuals, because for now very few of us save enough money for retirement. And it would be good for the country as a whole, because the money we save goes into the pile that business and the government borrow from. The money business borrows creates new products and services and jobs. The more money the U.S. Treasury can borrow from its

citizens, the less it will have to borrow overseas, so the less dependent the U.S. will be on investors in China, the Middle East, and elsewhere. And the argument against a consumption tax? Critics say there's no guarantee that such a tax will work comfortably in the real world. Suppose Washington adds a consumption tax without cutting the income tax? Also, a consumption tax might be harder on lower income people than on higher earners. Let's suppose necessities, such as food and medicine, were exempt from taxes. Is an air conditioner a necessity? Maybe not. Lower income people are more likely to buy a new air conditioner because the old one in the bedroom breaks down and they have little choice but to replace it, tax or no tax. Higher income folks might have a choice between buying an air conditioner for a room in a beach house or saving the money.

Who decides how to spend the money?

As with taxes, spending starts with Congress. After hearings and consultations with the Defense Department, the Agriculture Department, and the other departments and agencies of the federal government, Congress prepares a budget and sends it to the White House for the President's signature. The President has already had considerable influence on what is in the budget, of course, because he hires and fires the heads of all of those departments and agencies that have pleaded their cases before Congress. Frequently, Congress proposes less money than the President's people have requested, which is not surprising. What may seem harder to believe is that sometimes Congress gives some of those agencies more money than they asked for. Typically, a Congressman may represent a district in which a company makes tires for, say, an advanced jet fighter. The Pentagon may have decided that it has all the jet fighters that it needs. But the Congressman from the district where the tires are made wants the Pentagon to make more jets, as does the Congresswoman from the district where the tail struts are made, and so forth. So the struggle between the Congress and the White House goes on and on, until it is painfully resolved.

How can government spending increase GDP and employment?

In a recession the economy is performing at less than capacity, as the economists put it. Potential is going to waste. There are a lot of empty office buildings, shuttered hardware stores, abandoned coffee shops, and motorcycle factories reduced from three shifts a day to one. Most important, a lot of human brain and muscle power is just waiting around for work. So government has the option of spending money when private industry is not spending. That is called a stimulus. The object is to bring the economy closer to full capacity, to boost the GDP and employment. A paycheck is a paycheck whether it comes from a factory making motorcycles or a federal- or state-funded highway project building a bridge. If the contractor hires an additional pipefitter, she will take her paycheck and make her contribution to what is called the "multiplier effect." She spends a few dollars at the coffee shop, and the waitress uses her generous tip to help buy a present for her boyfriend. The owner of the gift shop uses the cash to buy groceries, and the grocer then buys flowers for his wife. So those few dollars from the pipefitter's paycheck swell in time into an expanding GDP.

Does it work?

In theory, perfectly. In practice, there are hitches. Let's take the bridge-building project we just mentioned. A stimulus is expected to work in a hurry. The road workers are sitting at home; their unemployment checks will end soon. But a bridge can't be planned and constructed in a rush. Engineering plans have to be drafted and approved. Pause for a lot of decision making. The bridge plan has to be coordinated with repairs on the existing highways on both ends. The bridge will have an impact on the river below. Have the environmental watchdogs signed off on the project yet?

Plenty of pipefitters and masons are ready and eager to work. But perhaps electricians and steamroller drivers are fully employed elsewhere. It often takes a long time for a stimulus project to get underway. Sometimes the recession that made it seem so urgent is a fading memory by the time it does. Assuming the bridge was actually necessary and not just a make-work project, that's not a terrible outcome. The new bridge is a worthwhile addition; it just didn't do anything to shove the economy out of recession.

Can government cut taxes to speed up the economy?

A tax cut is also a stimulus that can often put cash in people's hands faster than a spending project. The pipefitter gets her tax rebate check in the mail and right away buys a new lawnmower. The employed electrician has more cash in his next paycheck because the amount withheld for taxes has dropped; the electrician buys new power tools at the hardware store. Now the owner of the hardware store is even closer to his dream of buying a Harley Davidson. Again, the multiplier effect expands spending in the economy. But in some respects tax policy is a much clumsier way of ginning up the economy than government spending. Because the benefits of the tax cut go to the employed electrician and pipefitter as well as their unemployed colleagues, the total impact on unemployment is not as immediate. Maybe the pipefitter and the well-to-do dentist, who also receives a tax reduction, save the extra cash from lower taxes rather than spend it right away. There's nothing sinful in that, and much of the time government encourages such behavior—but not during a recession when the immediate goal is to have spending multiply through the economy fast and put people to work. Also, it is difficult politically to reverse tax policy, especially upwards. When the bridge is built, it's finished. No more spending on it. But even after a tax cut is no longer needed to fight recession, the tax cut might go on and on.

Can government increase taxes to slow down the economy?

Theoretically, yes. Raising taxes takes cash out of people's hands and slows down spending, the reverse of what lowering taxes does. But think about how difficult it is for government to raise taxes for that purpose. The situation in which the government would want to slow down the economy is one in which the economy is overheating; factories are running flat out; almost everyone is employed and has cash, and everyone competes with everyone else for bigger

homes and fancier vacations. The result is inflation. Prices rise. A possible remedy is for government to raise taxes and thereby reduce the amount of cash with which people compete and fuel inflation. But that would require politicians to tell voters squeezed by rising inflation that they, the politicians, are going to squeeze them even more by raising taxes as well. Politicians can be forgiven if they hesitate to raise taxes as a cure for an overstimulated economy.

What's the bottom line? Are government spending and taxing good ways to fix a troubled economy?

We've made the best case we can for both, and Congresses and Presidents are certainly going to go on clamoring for changes in spending and taxing as means for curing an ailing economy. Economists, however, are not enthusiastic by and large. Economists consider them clumsy instruments that are slow to take effect and sometimes have unintended consequences. Conservatives might argue that government help discourages the jobless from looking harder for work. Generally, economists prefer adjusting the money supply as a faster, surer way of either energizing a sluggish economy or calming an overactive one. We'll discuss the money supply in Chapter 5.

chapter 4
Getting into Debt

*It's been around from the beginning, but
the cause has become more worrisome*

INTRODUCTION

Debt is as American as barbeque ribs and corn whiskey. The nation was born in debt. At the end of the Revolutionary War both the Continental Congress and the former colonies owed huge debts to soldiers, to suppliers of horses, food, and ammunition, and to France, among others. The northern and middle states owed more than the southern, but in a deal ably negotiated by Alexander Hamilton in 1790, all of the debt was rolled into a single federal obligation. That was a break for the northerners. In exchange, the national capital was to be moved in time from New York to a spot closer to southern comfort, a swatch of land just across the Potomac River from Virginia. Through most of U.S. history and for reasons easy to understand, the debt rose during times of war and subsided afterward. The debt actually fell to zero for a time in the 1830s, and in the half century following the Civil War, the federal government managed to run surpluses in 36 years. The colossal strains of World War II pushed the debt to an extraordinary level. But in recent decades, a fundamental change has taken place. War is no longer the only force driving the national debt. Social programs now pile up huge expenses as well. Unlike wars, programs like Social Security and Medicare do not include an "exit strategy." How worried should we be?

What's the difference between deficit and debt?

The deficit is the shortfall during a single year between what the government spends and what it takes in through taxes and other receipts. Those other receipts are relatively small, but they include things like duties on some imported goods, the sale of government property, and the fees the government charges ranchers to graze their cattle on the expansive tracts of land the federal government owns in the West. Almost always the government spends more money than it takes in. For example, in the 65 years from the end of World War

II until 2010 the government ran a surplus in only 12 years. The accumulation of all the deficits over the years, minus the occasional surpluses, is the national debt, which in late 2011 was almost $11 trillion and growing. (Some of those who worry about the national debt use a figure that is several trillion dollars higher than that, but they include money the federal government owes itself. For example, the Treasury borrows money from the Social Security Trust Fund, which currently runs a surplus, to pay other bills.)

How can the U.S. spend more money than it takes in?

Simple. It does what individuals and companies and all kinds of organizations do: It borrows. It sells federal government notes, bills, and bonds, many to U.S. banks and insurance companies and other investors, but increasingly to foreign investors as well. The Chinese government, for example, recently owned $1.2 trillion of debt issued by the U.S. Treasury.

Q&A

Q

Should the government ever borrow?

A

Generally, economists and policy makers make the case that government should be saving money and paying down debt when the economy is booming and pulling in a lot of tax revenues. But borrowing isn't always bad, especially if the government is borrowing to build highways and bridges and schools and similar infrastructure projects. By increasing the capacity of the infrastructure those projects will promote economic growth. In a similar way it often makes sense for us as individuals to borrow to get advanced academic degrees that will increase our incomes and future well-being. The other circumstance in which there is a legitimate case for government borrowing is during a recession. Tax receipts automatically fall in a recession, and we certainly don't want to raise tax rates or cut government spending just as a recession begins. The government sometimes borrows and then spends the loan in a deliberate effort to stimulate the economy. If it works, that kind of borrowing will help the economy recover more quickly. Economists are by and large skeptical, however, that such borrowing and spending is necessarily effective in all circumstances, as we talked about in Chapter 3.

When is borrowing wrong?

Borrowing has very serious downsides. When the government goes into the marketplace to borrow money, it sometimes competes for that money with private borrowers, both individuals and corporations. The rule of supply and demand kicks in again, and interest rates rise. The higher rates discourage corporations from borrowing and investing in new businesses, from cereals to cell phones, that would create more jobs. The other bad effect is that an increase in government borrowing—at ever higher interest rates because of the competition—pushes up the amount of the federal budget that goes to paying interest to the lenders, do-mestic and foreign alike. More than 5% of the federal budget is now earmarked for paying interest on the debt. And here's a problem with borrowing that is not immediately obvious. When interest rates rise in the U.S., foreigners buy dollars to invest in U.S. bonds and other holdings that pay those high rates. Demand sends the value of the dollar up, which sounds great at first as goods and services made abroad will be less expensive for us. But it will mean that U.S. products will be more expensive for foreigners, because it will cost them more euros or yen to buy them. So U.S. exports will fall and imports will climb.

How much debt is too much?

Instead of thinking of it in terms of dollars, many economists say it is more useful to think of debt as a percentage of GDP. The two numbers—debt and GDP—are not directly dependent on each other, but their relative size is a handy way of thinking about debt. A debt of $11 trillion sounds like a lot of money—and it is—but it's only slightly more than 70% of our current GDP, a much lower debt rate than that of other industrial nations. (Greece's debt in the midst of a debt crisis has run to 150% of its GDP.) Most economists believe that the current amount of U.S. debt is tolerable. If GDP grows at a faster rate than the debt, no problem. What worries economists is that debt is going to grow faster than GDP, accelerating as Social Security and Medicare payments to an aging population grow bigger and bigger.

How long can the U.S. get away with this?

Impossible to say. Investors keep sending money to Washington because the U.S. economy is the world's biggest by far, and its government is not likely to crumble and refuse to pay its debts. But will that confidence continue forever? It was severely shaken in the summer of 2011 when Democrats and Republicans in Congress gridlocked on whether to raise the debt ceiling, the amount the federal government is allowed to borrow. Without additional borrowing, the government would not have been able to pay some of its bills including, perhaps, interest payments on its debt. Although the gridlock was ultimately broken and the ceiling raised, at some point lenders may lose their faith that the U.S. can make its interest payments. Borrowing could stop. U.S. taxes could soar, or services could plummet. Or both.

Do we need a balanced budget amendment to the Constitution?

Congressional legislation puts a limit on the amount that government can borrow, but Congress retains the power to increase the limit when it sees fit. From time to time some people have suggested an amendment to the Constitution — an edict that would be beyond Congress's power to fiddle with — that would require the budget to be balanced every year. All state constitutions except Vermont's have such provisions. But that would really hamstring the ability of Congress and the President to cope with a recession. A lot of government workers would be put on leave, offices closed, unemployment compensation slashed — all adding to the struggles of an already tired economy. Indeed, partly because of such balanced budget provisions, states, counties, and cities are forced to lay off teachers, social workers, firefighters, police officers, and others when tax revenues decline in a recession.

Q

So how do we get out of this mess?

There are three ways. The economy can grow so robustly that tax revenues will create a string of surpluses that will wipe out the string of deficits. Those surpluses did come through for a while in the late 1990s, when the economy was booming and taxes were relatively high. But that's not likely to happen again in the foreseeable future. The more realistic ways of reducing the debt are by raising taxes or cutting spending. Almost certainly, it will be necessary to do both. And both will be extremely difficult and painful. Even though U.S. federal income taxes currently are not very high by historic standards (the income tax became a permanent fixture in 1913), most of us now live in states with state income taxes, as well as real estate and sales taxes and more. So to many our tax burden seems high, even though our total taxes are low compared to those of most other developed nations. The country has developed such a reflex aversion to taxes that the slogan "no new taxes" has become the politicians' mantra. To cut spending is an equally agonizing and emotional task. Everyone has a favorite nominee for an easy cut, be it public broadcasting and the arts or the military. Yet every favorite target has a horde of reasonable, articulate defenders. Some years ago a candidate for the presidency maintained that he could balance the budget by eliminating "waste, fraud, and abuse." By all means, slaying those three devils is a worthy goal. But no one has come close to identifying enough of them to balance the budget.

Q&A

Q What are entitlements?

A

That's the spending that frightens economists and other experts the most. These days less than half of the federal government budget is what is called discretionary spending. Congress and the President, at their discretion, authorize spending and appropriate funds, after the kind of maneuvering and fighting that has been going on since the George Washington administration. What is striking is that these days less than half of the budget is determined in this fashion. The other half of the federal budget, slightly more than half actually—and growing—is mandatory spending. Congress and Presidents in the past have written laws establishing programs that they have promised to keep on funding. The money gets appropriated whether the sitting President and Congress specifically okay it or not. Although not strictly known as mandatory spending, interest on the federal debt, which we talked about earlier,

is a "must pay." Those who have made loans to the federal government get their money on schedule, because it is still hard to imagine—although no longer unthinkable—that the U.S. government would default on its debt payments. The biggest shares of mandatory spending are entitlement programs, especially Social Security, Medicare, and Medicaid. If you reach a certain age, you are entitled to Social Security as well as Medicare payments for your back surgery or angioplasty or whatever ails you; if you're poor you get Medicaid. You don't have to ask Congress for money the way the director of the FBI or the head of the EPA does. The reason those entitlement programs are frightening is that as people live longer, more and more need back surgery and angioplasty, and more and more wind up in nursing homes, where they spend all their money until they're poor and qualify for Medicaid.

Q

So will Social Security be eliminated?

A

That's unlikely. The program is too popular, not only with the elderly and near elderly, but also with their children, who don't want to wind up supporting old and indigent parents. Anyhow, Social Security isn't the real problem. Actuaries can predict with some accuracy how many of today's 30-year-olds, for example, are going to live until 95, and how much it will cost in Social Security payments to get them to that age. Payroll taxes can be increased moderately over the years to cover that payout, and people can be required to work longer before they can collect full benefits. Indeed that minimum age for full benefits, once 65, has been inching up for years. The far bigger threats are Medicare and Medicaid. Unlike Social Security, the Medicare program is open-ended and almost out of control. Generally, the longer people live, the sicker they get and the more care they are entitled to—

back surgery and chemotherapy and cataract removal and whatever else—without much restriction. In other industries, from making cars to making hotel reservations, computers, robots, and other technological advances tend to reduce costs. Medical technology, on the other hand, from kidney dialysis to heart transplants, may have performed miracles, but it has not saved money. More technology has led to more spending. The part of Medicaid that provides care for the failing elderly in nursing homes doesn't require much high-tech equipment, but it does demand a lot of expensive hands-on attention by nurses, psychiatrists, and others because many nursing home residents suffer from Alzheimer's and other forms of dementia. Unless the growth in medical care spending slows down, the debt will keep growing faster.

EASY **ECONOMICS**

chapter 5
The Fed

This very powerful institution
performs a kind of magic

INTRODUCTION

Every country has its "central bank," and the Federal Reserve is the central bank of the United States. The Fed is a nonprofit institution, part government agency, part private organization. Its primary role is to keep the economy moving ahead on an even keel.

Historically, the Fed has operated cautiously and behind closed doors, in the belief that any sudden moves could destabilize stock and bond markets and the economy in general. But the Fed stepped up to the 2007–2009 financial crisis with a series of bold initiatives, which included bailing out struggling banks by relieving them of their "toxic" debt—loans with high risk of default. Those measures were controversial and brought the institution into the public glare. The Fed's doings, long an obsession with Wall Street, have now drawn the attention of Main Street. If you are a Main Streeter, chances are you have questions about what the Fed does and why it is important.

If the Federal Reserve can't prevent bank failures, who needs it?

We do. While banks failed in the 2007–2009 financial crisis, many more survived, as did the financial system as a whole, thanks in part to the intervention of the Fed. In any case, preventing widespread bank failures is only one of the Fed's jobs—not even the most important one.

Q&A

So what does the Fed do?

Three things:

1. To prevent panics and failures, the Fed regulates banking practices and makes money available to banks when they come up short. It does this by providing loans through a facility known as the "discount window," which in the old days was a real window but isn't any-more. The discount window doesn't offer what we commonly think of as "discounts," either, but lends to banks when they lack the funds to meet unexpected demand from depositors and borrowers. Discount lending is routine—not to be confused with a bailout!

2. The Fed performs various behind-the-scenes housekeeping duties that keep the banking system humming. These tasks include, among other things, check clearing, processing electronic payments, holding our federal tax dollars until the government is ready to spend them, and moving currency around the country to meet the needs of local banks. Somebody's got to do it!

3. But its most important job is the setting and implementing of monetary policy.

What's monetary policy?

Through its monetary policy, the Fed attempts to control the amount of money and credit available to consumers and businesses. "Attempts" is key, since the Fed does its best to influence economic conditions, but cannot dictate them outright. The economy has a mind of its own. Monetary policy is one of two tools that the government uses to try to manage the economy, steering it toward growth and full employment and away from recession and inflation. The other tool is fiscal policy, which is covered in Chapter 3. Most economic policy debates center on whether the government has gone too far or not far enough in using these tools.

Why not just make as much money available as people want?

Because too much money chasing after a limited supply of goods and services will drive prices up. That's inflation, and when it occurs, our dollars buy less. The Fed needs to walk a fine line, making enough money available to promote economic growth, but not so much as to cause inflation. Monetary policy aims to smooth out the peaks and valleys in the business cycle, while at the same time encouraging the economy to grow.

When recession is a threat, making more money available leads to lower interest rates. Interest rates are the "price" of money, and will naturally decline when money is more abundant, thanks to the law of supply and demand. Consumers then use increased money and borrowing power to buy more homes, cars, and other things, and that, in turn, leads to more jobs and higher wages. Meanwhile, because business can borrow at lower cost, it becomes more profitable to pursue new ventures. New products and services come on the market, generating even more employment.

But once the economy is producing as much as it can and unemployment is very low, any further increase in the availability of money will cause prices to increase. If that starts to happen, the Fed may decide to shrink the amount of money available—or more often, slow its rate of growth. Then, interest rates rise and people borrow and spend less, taking pressure off prices.

How does the Fed set monetary policy?

1. The Federal Open Market Committee (FOMC) determines monetary policy. It decides the amount of money and credit that should be available at any given time. It is one of three components of what is properly known as the Federal Reserve System. The other two are the Federal Reserve Board and the network of 12 regional Federal Reserve Banks.

The Federal Reserve Board, composed of seven Governors, with one appointed as Chairman, presides over the Fed's head office, which is located in Washington, D.C. The U.S. President appoints the Governors, with the approval of the Senate, but they are relatively free of political pressure in their decision-making. One reason: The Governors enjoy long terms in office—14 years.

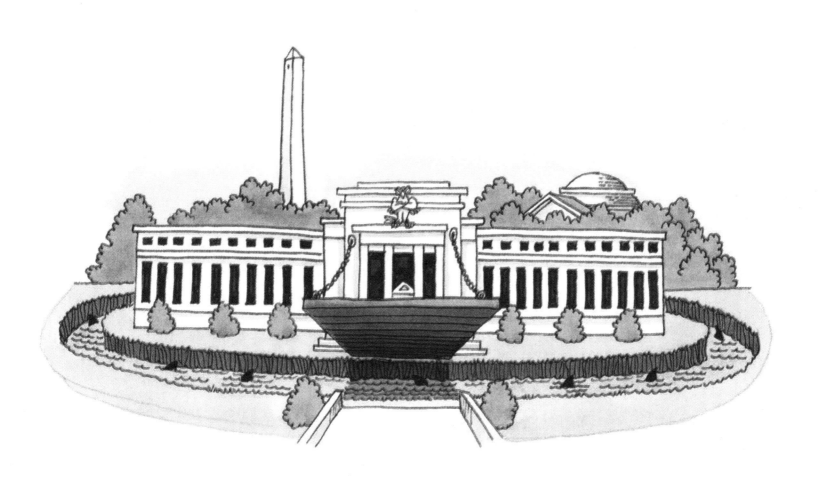

2. The 12 regional Federal Reserve Banks monitor local economic conditions and perform many of the Fed's housekeeping tasks. Each bank has its own president, appointed by a board made up of local bankers and other business and community leaders.

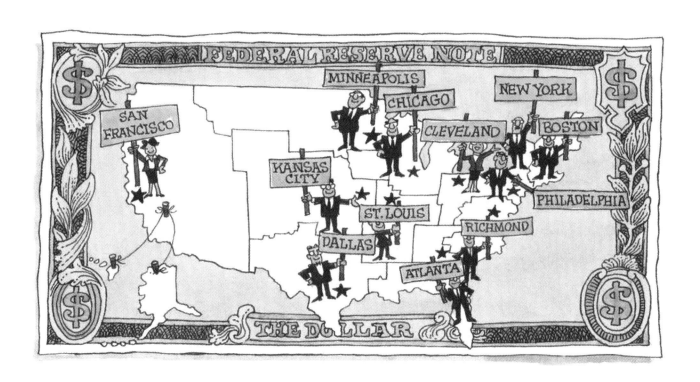

3. The FOMC, which meets in Washington, D.C., is made up of the seven Governors who serve on the Federal Reserve Board and the presidents of five of the regional Federal Reserve Banks. Very little is "open" about the Federal Open Market Committee. It's the inner sanctum of the Fed and its deliberations, usually held eight times a year, are not public. The committee, however, is more transparent now than it has ever been, releasing partial minutes three weeks after it meets.

How does the Fed increase and decrease the amount of money available in the economy?

By buying and selling government bonds. These are not the U.S. savings bonds you buy through payroll deductions but the Treasury securities that are constantly traded in the bond market and held by investors all over the world. When the Fed pays for the bonds it buys, it adds money to the economy. And when the Fed takes in money from the sale of bonds, the amount of money in the economy is reduced.

One of the 12 regional banks is the Federal Reserve Bank of New York, and it is first among equals. It carries out the monetary policy established by the FOMC by buying and selling government bonds on Wall Street. Incidentally, the New York Fed also holds the world's largest gold hoard in its basement vault. Most of the gold, which is in the form of bars, belongs to other countries and is used to settle international transactions. Each country is assigned an individual cage, and when gold changes ownership, bars are physically moved from one cage to another. For more on international payments, see Chapter 7.

Q&A

Where does the Fed get the money to buy bonds?

Okay, brace yourself; this is a hard concept to get your mind around: It creates it, out of nothing.

In other words, the Fed prints money to buy the bonds?
It doesn't need to. It can create "invisible" money. To grasp this, you need to know how economists define "money." The so-called "money supply" is much more than the bills and coins in circulation. It is the sum of all currency—bills and coins—plus bank deposits.

Bank deposits are "invisible" in that they exist only as entries on banks' books. When you deposit money in your checking or savings account, it doesn't sit as a pile of greenbacks in the bank's vault until you withdraw it.

Even if you make the deposit in cash, as opposed to a check or electronic funds transfer, the bank will hang on to little or none of that cash. It credits your account on its books, and the physical money you handed to the teller is used by the bank for other transactions.

Normally, all the bank's depositors don't demand all their deposits at the same time, so the bank can get by with a limited amount of cash on hand. But in the rare event that a lot of depositors want their money, the result is the catastrophe known as a bank run (but remember that the bank can get help from the discount window).

Bank deposits constitute a much larger part of the money supply than bills and coins. Currency, in fact, is just the tip of the monetary iceberg. The government circulates only enough of it to meet the day-to-day cash needs of individuals and businesses. Most of the money out there is in bank accounts, not wallets.

The Fed creates new money by creating new bank deposits. When it buys bonds, the Fed simply issues a check (or the electronic equivalent) that is backed by nothing at all. It doesn't draw on funds in any account. If you or I tried this, we'd land in jail, but because it has the legal authority to create money, the Fed can get away with it. The check is honored by the seller's bank, and the sale price is credited to the seller's account.

Q&A

So the Fed doesn't print money?

Not in order to add new money to the economy and technically, not at all. It's not the Fed but the U.S. Mint, which is part of the Treasury Department, that is in charge of the printing presses. That said, when the Fed expands the invisible portion of the money supply, a side effect is the increased production of currency by the U.S. Mint.

It's the Treasury's job to print as much currency as is needed for the smooth conduct of cash transactions. Imagine shopkeepers unable to make change and empty ATMs—how annoying is that? Increased bank deposits inevitably lead to more economic activity and additional cash transactions. Result: When the Fed expands bank deposits, the U.S. Mint revs up its presses.

How does the Fed destroy money?

If you haven't yet shaken the idea that money equals currency, you probably think that destroying money means burning it or running it through a giant shredder. Not. When the Fed wants to reduce the money supply, it sells bonds, collecting money from buyers who pay for the bonds out of their bank deposits. The buyer's bank account is reduced by the sale price, but the Fed doesn't stash the money away somewhere for future use. The money just disappears.

But where does it go?

It doesn't go anywhere. Remember, it's not paper money. When the money no longer appears on any bank's books, it no longer exists. To borrow from Monty Python's famous dead parrot sketch, "The money is no more! It has ceased to be! It is ex-money!"

Q&A

How does the Fed's buying bonds on Wall Street increase the amount
of money in the pockets of ordinary consumers and businesses?

The sale proceeds are rattled through the U.S. banking system, and that not only spreads the money around, but creates even more of it. When the Fed buys bonds, the sellers deposit the proceeds at their banks. Fed rules require banks to keep a fraction—usually 10%—of their deposits in reserve, either as cash in their vaults or, more often, in accounts they can tap at the Fed. The bank is free to issue loans equal to the remaining 90% and will usually do so, since lending is how banks make their profits. Note that 100% is still on deposit

and available to the depositor should he elect to withdraw it. The bank creates the money it lends. Whether the Fed is buying or selling, the reserve requirements magnify the impact of the transaction. When the Fed buys a bond, for example, it sets off a chain reaction of loans that ultimately generate much more new money than the original purchase. Here's how it works:

1. The FOMC directs the New York Fed to add money to the economy.

2. The New York Fed goes shopping on Wall Street, buying bonds from major financial firms that have been selected to serve as dealers. To pay for the bonds, the Fed issues checks (or the electronic equivalent), say for $1,000, if that is what the Fed paid for the bonds. Those checks will become new money when they are deposited.

3. The dealers are domestic firms like Citigroup, Goldman Sachs, JPMorgan Chase, and Merrill Lynch. Foreign-based financial companies— Barclays, Deutsche Bank, Mizuho Securities, and Nomura Securities—also serve those roles. As these dealers deposit these checks in their bank accounts, the banks record increases of $1,000 in deposits and in reserves.

4. In each case, 10% is required to be kept as part of the bank's reserves, enabling the bank to lend an amount equal to 90% of the deposited amount, or $900. Since the original $1,000 is still on deposit, the $900 in loan proceeds is more new money—money created out of nothing. A total of $1,900 of new money is now available in the economy.

5. But the process doesn't end there. It continues, as the borrower spends the money she's borrowed. That is the purpose of the monetary policy. The goal was to encourage individuals and businesses to spend, with the ultimate goal of increasing GDP, employment, and incomes.

Q&A

6. The payee deposits the $900 sale proceeds in his bank. Once again, reserves and deposits increase. This time by $900. The bank will have to keep 10% in its reserves, but can make a new loan with the rest.

7. An amount equal to 90% of the deposited $900 becomes available for lending. A new $810 loan is more new money, bringing the total of available new money so far to $2,710—the original $1,000 plus the new $900 loan and then the now available $810 loan. All the increases in loans are increases in deposits and increases in the money supply.

And so on and so on and so on ... until the original $1,000 purchase of bonds has expanded the money supply by $10,000. Sweet.

Q&A

Does the Fed's selling government bonds on Wall Street decrease the amount of money in the pockets of ordinary consumers and businesses?

Now here's how it works in reverse:

When the Fed wants to calm an overheated economy, it will reduce the number of bonds it purchases. Then, the money supply will continue to grow but will do so at a slower pace. On rare occasions, however, the Fed may feel the need to shrink the money supply, and

that throws the process into reverse. Once again, reserve requirements magnify the impact:

1. The FOMC directs the New York Fed to subtract money from the economy.

2. The New York Fed holds an auction, selling government bonds to the same group of dealers. If the dealers aren't interested, the Fed lowers the prices of the bonds. Each bond pays a fixed dollar amount of interest and that means that if the price one has to pay falls, the actual interest rate on the bond increases. And that higher interest rate will eventually make those bonds more attractive.

3. The dealers withdraw money from their bank accounts to pay for the bonds they buy. Usually they sell those bonds to their customers, and those customers pay for the bonds by withdrawing money from their accounts. In either case, the purchases of bonds will mean reductions in either the dealers' or their customers' bank deposits and reserves by the same amounts that they have paid for the bonds.

4. The money the Fed receives for the bonds simply ceases to exist. Bank reserves disappear. Bank deposits decline. Banks cannot make new loans when old loans are paid off, as they do not have sufficient reserves to support those loans. The money supply grows smaller.

How does the Fed influence interest rates?

It can raise or lower the rate it charges at its discount window, which should prompt banks to raise or lower their rates to customers. But mainly, it influences rates through its manipulation of the money supply: When the Fed increases bank reserves and banks are able to make more loans, they lower their interest rates in an effort to attract customers. And when the Fed tightens up the money supply, banks can charge more for the few loans they make, so they raise their rates.

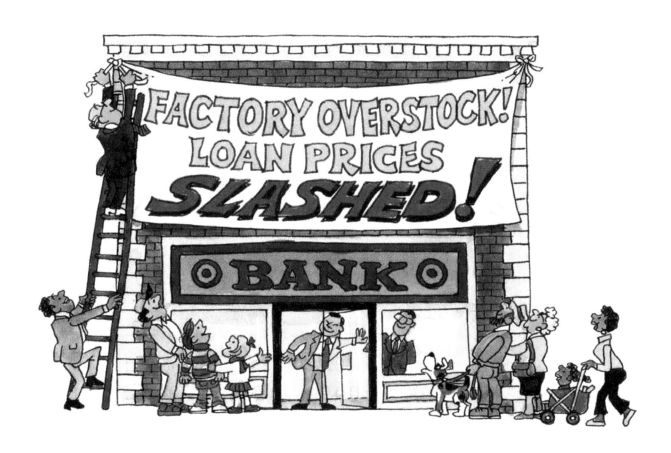

Q&A

What's the Fed funds rate?

That's the interest rate on which the Fed's tinkering with reserves has the most immediate impact. It's the rate banks charge when they lend reserves to one another. Like discount window lending, these overnight loans serve to smooth over short-term shortfalls. When reserves increase, the Fed funds rate drops, and vice versa. The Fed funds rate sets the pace for all short-term rates, including those on money market funds. It is also called the interbank lending rate. The FOMC sets targets for this rate when it instructs bond traders at the New York Fed to add to bank reserves by buying bonds or to subtract from bank reserves by selling bonds. When bond trading brings the Fed funds rate in line with its target rate, the money supply has reached the level where the Fed wants it.

Does the Fed have any control over rates on longer loans, such as car loans and mortgages?

1. Some. Longer-term rates in general tend to move in step with short-term rates. But other forces may come into play, weakening the Fed's grip. A type of chart called the yield curve can show the effects of these other forces.

Under normal circumstances, long-term rates are higher than short-term rates because lenders are not willing to part with their money for long time periods without additional compensation.

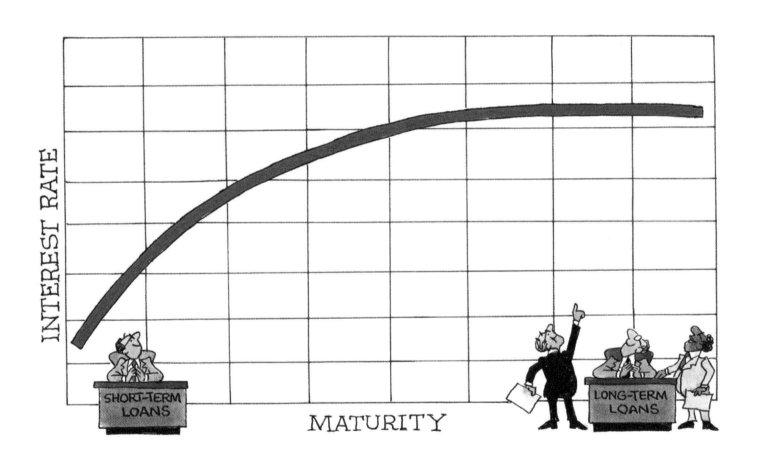

2. When the Fed hikes short-term rates, longer-term rates tend to rise in tandem.

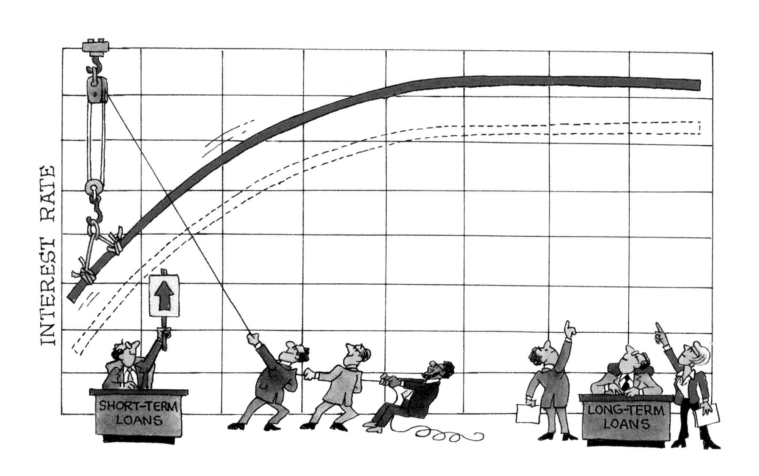

3. But higher short-term rates may not lead to higher long-term rates if, for example, the economy appears to be cooling. Lenders will then be satisfied with relatively low long-term rates because they fear long-term rates will soon go even lower. Slower growth or recession eventually leads to lower rates across the board, as borrowing and spending decline.

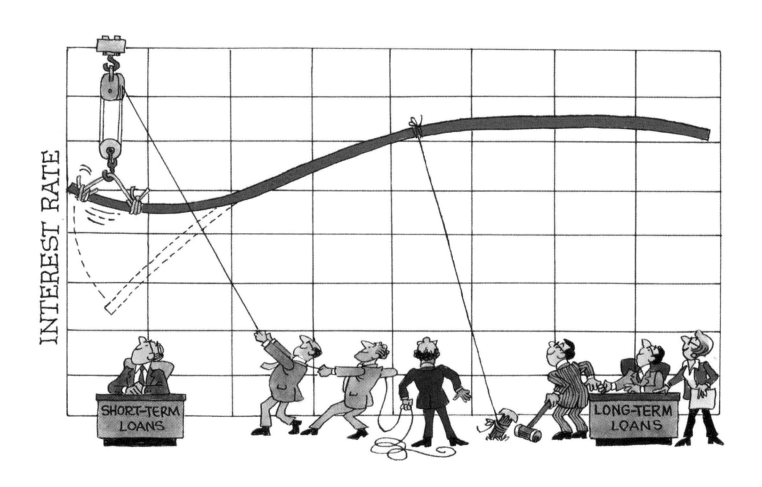

INTEREST RATE

SHORT-TERM LOANS

LONG-TERM LOANS

4. Similarly, lower short-term rates won't drag long-term rates down if lenders smell serious inflation ahead. Lenders will continue to demand high long-term rates to offset the risk that higher prices will erode the value of the loan principal by the time it has been repaid.

EASY **ECONOMICS**

chapter 6
High-Flying Finance

*The Wall Street elite can make
the planet tremble*

INTRODUCTION

Finance probably began a few thousand years ago when some humans crawled out of lives of bare subsistence and crafted the beginnings of commerce. A farmer knew he would have customers for the wheat he wanted to grow, if only he could get the seed and fertilizer he needed. So someone provided those ingredients, likely in exchange for part of the crop. That was primitive finance. Similarly, a trader knew he could sell the local wine to guzzlers across the sea if someone would provide the wine in exchange for part of the shipload of spices and fabrics the trader would bring back with him. That, too, was a form of finance. Although finance has grown more complex with loans, stocks, bonds, warrants, puts, calls, swaps, options, futures, and on and on in the mind-numbing profusion of what are called in the trade "financial instruments," those fundamentals are still around. Party A needs money up front to plant a field, build a house, start a catering business, or launch a commercial space shuttle. Party B, who could be a banker, a rich heir, a labor union, a college endowment, a mutual fund, or one of many other kinds of investors, is willing to put up the money in the expectation of making a good profit. That's finance. In these days of high-flying finance, those agreements are surrounded by all kinds of dizzying side bets and after bets.

Who were the first financiers?

The first people who were formally considered financiers may have been early Romans who came up with the idea of selling shares of ownership (stock, or equity) in enterprises; Renaissance Italians seem to have invented bonds, that is, pieces of paper representing loans. In the early days of the U.S., commercial banks were behind much of finance, which was simple and limited to a relatively few customers. Ordinary citizens generally were not able to go to banks or savings and loan associations to borrow money to buy a house. That came much later. (Even in the early 20th century, fewer than half of Americans owned their own homes; those who

had mortgages had to put down as much as 50% of the purchase price and they had to pay off the mortgage in six to eight years). In the beginning, banks were mostly for businesses. Bankers tended to be extremely cautious about to whom they lent and for how long. To make sure they had enough cash available to meet unexpected demands from depositors, bankers generally made only short-term loans, good for 30 to 60 days. Typically, manufacturers and shopkeepers would use these funds to pay their suppliers and workers until they could sell the goods to customers. Small businesses still rely to a large extent on bank loans.

Q&A

How did Wall Street and big-time finance get started?

While bankers took care of the financing needs of much of the country, some ambitious New Yorkers (encouraged by Alexander Hamilton) were trying to make their city a financial center, modeled on the great centers in cities like London and Paris. On May 17, 1792, a group of 24 stockbrokers and merchants gathered under a buttonwood tree at 68 Wall Street and drew up a constitution for buying and selling shares of ownership, or stock, in businesses, just as Europeans had long been doing. Early stocks were issued by a federal bank to raise money to pay off Revolutionary War debt. In time the members of this financial elite, holders of the right to trade stock, became the New York Stock Exchange. The business of buying and selling stocks and bonds began modestly and exploded into prominence with the great expansion of the railroads around the time of the Civil War. The reason is clear enough. Laying track across great stretches of land and manufacturing the engines and cars to fill the track was horrendously expensive. To finance it, railways sold stocks and bonds in great volumes.

How do big companies finance themselves today?

The investment bank was created to advise corporations on a range of crucial financial issues. Imagine, for example, a fictitious company we'll call Big Wheels (BW), a successful manufacturer of long-distance buses. BW has decided it wants to expand into the business of making cars for high-speed railway systems. BW calls in its investment banker for advice on how to come up with $1 billion to begin the new venture. The investment banker draws up a list of the alternatives. BW can raise the money by issuing more stock or issuing more bonds. If it decides to issue new stock, the investment bank will assemble a network of dealers, basically stock brokers, to sell the stock to the public. Or, the investment bank might locate a company already in the high-speed rail

business for BW to acquire or maybe merge with. That's the traditional role of the investment bank, the gentlemanly, well-paid, advisor. More recently, however, investment banks' biggest profits have come from buying and selling stocks and bonds apart from their clients' needs. If BW sells new stock to the public, the investment bank will keep some of that stock as payment for its services. The bank can hold onto those shares, sell them, or trade them and stretch their holdings into myriad investments. People who run investment banks are by and large extremely smart and have a much better sense than most other earthlings of how markets operate and where profits can be made. They can sometimes overreach, as they did in the financial crisis of 2007–2009.

How do new high-tech companies get financed?

Begin at the opposite end of the business spectrum from Big Wheels. Imagine a company called Small Paddles (SP). It's so small it isn't even a company yet, just an idea that a couple of young geniuses at Cal Tech have for a cheap engine for commercial space travel. They first raise some money from friends and family and perhaps from an "angel," or wealthy individual, to get started. Then, SP seeks out the attention of venture capitalists , who collect money from rich individuals, university endowment funds, hedge funds, and others to invest in just such opportunities as SP offers. There's a chance for those investors to get a terrific return (there's also a big risk for them to lose their whole investment). If and when SP's new engine progresses beyond an idea and into a prototype or product ready for market, the venture capitalists will team up with an investment bank, which will sell shares to the public, just as it did for Big Wheels. As this is the first time SP shares have been sold, it is called an initial public offering, an IPO.

Q&A

Q What caused the financial crisis of 2007–2009?

A Big question. The short answer is a lot of greed and stupidity, lack of regulation, the creation of complex financial products, lazy research, a measure of misplaced good intentions and much more. Entire books have been written to explain it, and many more will undoubtedly follow. Here we will just touch on a few of the forces at work and not in any particular order of importance. Interest rates were low in that decade, which made it easy to borrow. Some critics blame Alan Greenspan, then chairman of the Fed, for keeping interest rates too low for too long. Investors large and small could borrow money and put it in the stock market or elsewhere. Investment advisors commonly promised "above average returns," a phrase that brings to mind the description of Lake Wobegon as a place where the children are all above average. But in a world awash in money it was challenging to find investments that paid off handsomely; the supply of money was big, the demand for it so-so. Many investment opportunities had evaporated when the dot.com bubble ballooned and burst, largely because of dizzy ideas like www.walkyourkangaroo.com. That's a made-up service, of course, but some real ones were almost as absurd. Financiers were hungry for new opportunities. At the same time, well-meaning legislators and other good-hearted folks were urging banks to stretch their imaginations and their standards to make home mortgage loans to the subprime market, that is, to people who could not have dreamed of buying homes when interest rates were high. As money poured into the real estate market, the prices of homes ascended at awe-inspiring rates. Homeowners borrowed against those rising values with home equity loans (the same thing as second mortgages, but they don't sound like you're getting deeper into debt). In previous years a local banker would have balked at giving a $500,000 mortgage to a handyman with an annual income of $25,000. But what if the banker could sell that mortgage to another investor?

The banker would no longer have to worry about whether the handyman could make his monthly payment or not. So mortgage brokers, commercial bankers, investment bankers, and others created mortgage-backed securities, a pile of mortgages, many of them subprime and very risky, tied up in a bundle. The securities were attractive because they offered a high rate of return, and their risk was supposedly offset by diversification. Some homeowners would get in over their heads and default, but surely not battalions of them. The real estate market might go south in one region, but the real estate market had not fallen nationwide in many years. Unfortunately, battalions did eventually default, partly because they were misled by lenders about what the real costs of paying a mortgage would be, and partly because they deceived themselves. Many believed that the values of their homes would rise forever, so they could keep refinancing. The crisis went national. There were a lot of direct losers, both overreaching homeowners and overreaching investors. And there were enormous indirect losers, including the U.S. economy, which was pounded into its worst recession since the Great Depression.

What is leverage?

Leverage uses borrowing to magnify, or lift, the profits on an investment. But be warned: When the investment goes bad, borrowing also magnifies the losses. Let's say an insurance company, or any other institution or private investor, puts $100,000 of its own money into a project and earns 7%, or $7,000. Imagine also that the insurance company borrows $900,000 from others and invests that money in the same project at 7% as well. The insurance company's deal requires that it pay its lenders only 5%. Let's do the math. The insurance company takes in $70,000 (7% of $1 million). But it only has to pay its lenders $45,000 (5% of $900,000).

So it makes a net profit of $25,000 on its $100,000 investment—a very attractive return of 25%. Leverage is a sweet deal. But now imagine the worst. The economy weakens and the investment's pay-off declines to 4% from the original 7%. The insurance company is not simply making less money ($40,000 compared to $70,000); it is losing money, because it still has to pay its lenders $45,000. The lenders are scared. They want their money back now and ask that it be returned. Others refuse to offer more loans. Similar crises have been experienced thousands of times throughout an economy that is falling apart.

How do you "short" a stock?

You "short" a stock because you think its value is going to decline. Imagine that the stock of Big Wheels, which we mentioned earlier, is selling at $100 a share. You think the company is overrated, that it can't succeed in the high-speed rail business and that in the next few months the rest of the investment community is going to wise up as well. So you borrow 1,000 shares of BW, perhaps from a university endowment fund, and promise to return 1,000 shares in six months; you pay the endowment fund a fee for the privilege of borrowing its stock—and sell the stock, pocketing $100,000. Then you hope very hard that BW stock drops. If it falls to $80, say, you buy 1,000 shares and give them to the en-

dowment fund; you have made $20,000. Now imagine that instead of declining, BW's stock starts to rise. You and other "shorts" (people who short stocks) perspire a lot. It could turn out that you are going to have to buy BW stock at $120 a share. In that case you will have lost $20,000. Some in the investment community revile shorts as malignant speculators and predators. During the financial crisis of 2007–2009 at least one firm accused shorts of precipitating its collapse by spreading rumors. But there was little evidence for that. Shorts, moreover, perform a service. Their research often turns up bad news about a company's fundamentals that cheerleaders would prefer to ignore.

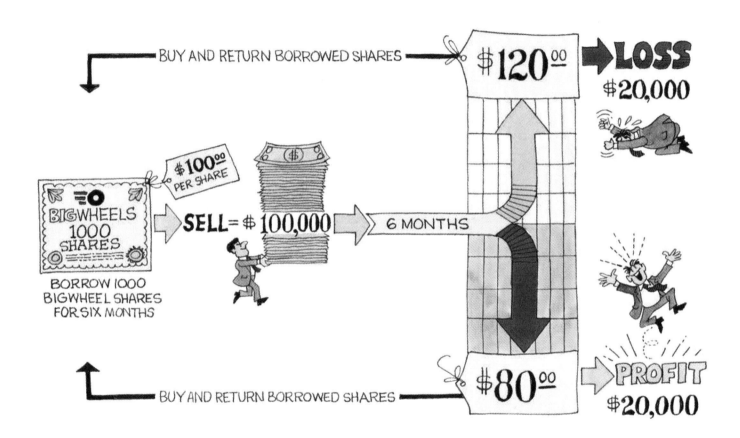

BUY AND RETURN BORROWED SHARES

$120.00 ➡ LOSS $20,000

$100.00 PER SHARE

BIGWHEELS 1000 SHARES

SELL = $100,000

6 MONTHS

BORROW 1000 BIGWHEEL SHARES FOR SIX MONTHS

BUY AND RETURN BORROWED SHARES

$80.00 ➡ PROFIT $20,000

What are hedge funds?

They are mutual funds for small groups of wealthy people and institutions, including at times pension funds and university endowments, that are willing and able to go beyond the bounds of conventional investing. They turn over their money to very clever managers who often specialize in narrow categories, such as emerging economies in South Asia, or exchange-rate fluctuations, or oil and gas exploration, and therefore find opportunities that the rest of us miss. Membership in these funds is limited to people and institutions with a lot of money who are presumably sophisticated and understand what they are getting into—and can withstand substantial losses even if they don't. This is why the Securities and Exchange Commission and other regulators allow hedge fund managers considerable latitude to use complex strategies, such as leverage, short selling, and derivatives (discussed later in this chapter), to enhance returns and manage risk.

What are private equity funds?

As with hedge funds, membership is restricted to the wealthy. But they have a different strategy. Hedge funds don't try to manage the enterprises they invest in. Private equity funds do. Typically, they buy a controlling interest in a troubled but promising publicly traded company, and fix it up like an old house. That often requires firing the old management and reducing the work force. When the company is healthy, that is, profitable, they flip it by selling the company back to the public, just as you might flip an old house that you repaired and then sold to someone else.

What are derivatives?

A These are fancy agreements whose value derives from something else, like a company stock that underlies the derivative. Here are a couple of examples: Instead of buying Hewlett-Packard stock, you decide to buy a "call" on Hewlett-Packard; this is an option—a derivative—entitling you to buy HP for a specified time at a specified price. From then on, the value of your derivative is going to be determined by what happens to the price of HP stock. If the HP stock goes up well beyond that specified price, you can make a lot of money, because you have to pay only the specified price. If the price of HP stock falls, the call is worthless and you lose the relatively small amount of money you paid for it.

Companies sometimes use derivatives as insurance policies. Airlines, for example, are at the mercy of fuel prices, which can gyrate wildly and often determine whether an airline makes or loses money for the year. So airlines buy forward fuel contracts, that is, they buy the right to purchase fuel at a specified price during a specified period. That takes a lot of heart-stopping anxiety out of the business. They know what fuel will cost them and can price their tickets accordingly. The value of that contract will fluctuate with the price of oil. When you hear people talk about swaps, options, calls, puts, forwards, they are talking about derivatives.

Q&A

Q Why do derivatives have a bad name?

A

Although they can serve a useful purpose—acting as insurance policies for airlines, for example—they can also be used by high-stakes gamblers and have tremendous power to throw markets into turmoil. Derivatives don't necessarily remain in the hands of the people who initiated them. They are bought and sold in markets. Millions of derivatives based on swings in currency exchange rates, wheat prices, and many other items are constantly changing hands. Not all of those markets are well regulated. During the subprime mortgage frenzy of the early 2000s, AIG, one of the world's biggest insurance companies, issued a derivative called a credit default swap, an insurance policy on mortgage-backed securities. If you bought a security that depended on homeowners paying their mortgages, you could also buy a credit default swap, which would pay

you if the homeowners defaulted. But you didn't have to own a mortgage-backed security to buy a credit-default swap. And some farsighted investors bet wisely that a lot of homebuyers with shaky incomes were in over their heads. Those shrewd investors bought huge amounts of credit default swaps, which is a little like buying fire insurance on your neighbors' homes and then hoping they go up in a blaze. Sure enough, the defaults came on like a raging forest fire. AIG had to pay off the holders of the credit default swaps, with claims so huge that they threatened to ruin AIG. If AIG had collapsed, insurance policies for many thousands of companies worldwide would have been worthless, and the entire financial system could have collapsed. The U.S. government bailed out AIG by buying most of its stock and giving it lines of credit.

Q&A

Q

What's a speculative bubble?

A

That's when the price of an asset—and an asset is just about anything you can own, from corporate bonds to racehorses—rises beyond what is rational. The tricky part is defining rational. A past chairman of the Fed, Alan Greenspan, was fond of saying that he acknowledged that there are bubbles. But, he added, they can be recognized only after they burst. Fair enough. But there are some hints that an asset might be bubbling. For example, over time the prices of homes will be determined by incomes. So when housing prices climb much faster than incomes, as they did during the 1990s, watch out for the burst. A widening spread between incomes and prices cannot go on forever. Similarly, over many decades the average prices of shares on U.S. stock exchanges have fluctuated at about 15 times earnings. (If securities analysts expect a company to earn $3 per share this year and its stock is selling on the market at $45 a share it has a price/earnings ratio of 15.) If large numbers of stocks, not just a promising star or two in an industry, sell for, say, 30 or 40 times earnings over a long period of time, beware. History warns that the prices will eventually crash.

EASY **ECONOMICS**

chapter 7
Globalization

Nowhere to hide: Everywhere is connected to everywhere else

INTRODUCTION

The world used to be so simple, so understandable—so local. Cars came from Detroit. Beef came from the Farm Belt. Grapefruit came from Florida. Baseball players came from pretty much the same places. Television sets and blue jeans, two great American inventions, were actually made in the U.S.A. Your company didn't lose work to a machine tool maker in Taiwan. . . . On the other hand, some pretty cool stuff was missing back then. Italian suits were hard to come by. Playroom games were boring until the Japanese applied electronics; and motorcycles were expensive. Nobody had heard of Indian or Thai restaurants, two great retreats for inexpensive dining. And who would have looked after your mother with as much care as that nurse's aide from Ghana does today? . . . Globalization. Do we hate it? Do we love it?

Q&A

Q What is globalization?

A

It has cultural and political meanings as well, but as far as economics is concerned, globalization is the growing trend for local economies in even the most remote spots of the world to be connected directly or indirectly with every other spot in the world. They are connected above all by trade that reaches just about every nook and cranny of the earth. Tourists venture from the rich world to the developing world, while laborers migrate from the developing world to the rich in search of livelihoods. Turkish workers in Germany or Filipinos in the U.S. send the euros and dollars they earn back home. That sort of globalization has been going on for centuries, perhaps millennia, sometimes in the form of barter, but it is more frequent and intense now. Globe-hopping combinations are endless. A Brazilian farmer drives an a U.S.-made harvester to gather soybeans that will be exported to India to feed office workers who will staff call centers in Bangalore to handle questions from credit card customers living in the U.S. Or, consider Boeing, as American an enterprise as ever there was—so you would think—with headquarters in Chicago and manufacturing, or at least assembling, near Seattle and elsewhere in the U.S. But typical of Boeing planes, the parts of the Boeing 787 were made in dozens of places outside the U.S. The floor beams came from India; the passenger doors from France; the crew escape door from Sweden; horizontal stabilizers from Italy; parts of the wings from Japan; and wing tips from South Korea. The initial customer for the plane was Tokyo's All Nippon Airways. Like other international airlines that buy 787s, ANA will fly passengers from nation to nation to spend their money, or make their money, in places far from home. Now that's globalization.

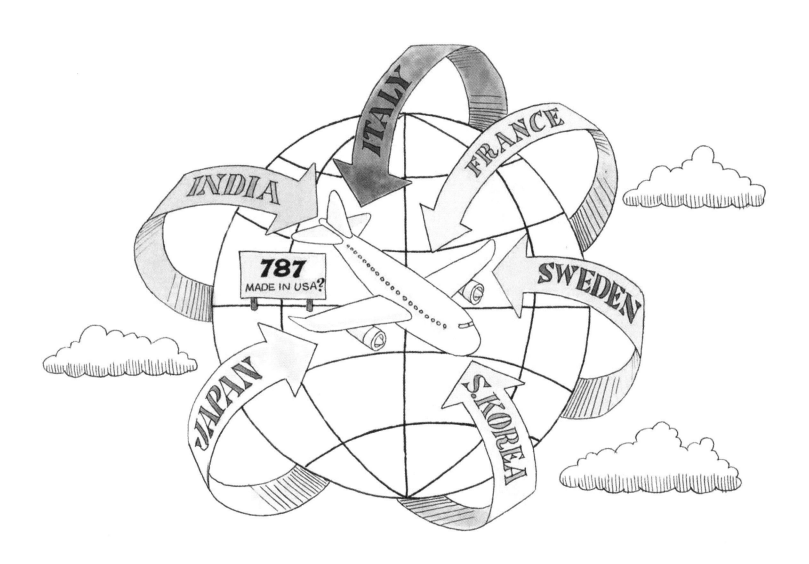

787
MADE IN USA?

INDIA

ITALY

FRANCE

SWEDEN

JAPAN

S.KOREA

Can Americans own and operate companies overseas?

Yes, a big component of globalization is something called foreign direct investment. U.S. investors, and for that matter investors from anywhere, can put a substantial amount of money into enterprises outside their own countries and demand an active role in running them. When General Motors builds a factory in China or Walmart builds a store in Mexico, that's direct investment. GM and Walmart own the property. And any of us can buy shares of stock in Toyota or a European design house—a different type of investment, as we aren't going to have a voice in running those companies.

What are financial and capital flows?

Those can be oceans of money washing from one nation to another, often with enormous consequences. It's a natural economic process for the most part. Investors, whether they are private groups or nations piloting what are called sovereign wealth funds, ship their money to where they are going to get greatest returns. China buys piles of U.S. Treasury notes, or Saudi Arabia lends billions to real estate developers in Spain. As a result, the lenders then have their hands close to the throats of the borrowers, theoretically at least, if they ask for their money back or stop buying bonds. What if the Chinese get frightened by the huge U.S. debt and refuse to buy any more Treasuries, except at sky-high interest rates? At the same time, the borrowers have their hands at the throats of the lenders in a similar way. If the Chinese, for example, were to act in a way that would drive down the value of U.S. Treasuries and make them seem very risky, the Chinese would suffer tremendous losses in the value of their portfolios. So this is a system that contains significant benefits—and terrors—for both sides.

Q&A

Q Is globalization good or bad?

A

That's the multi-trillion dollar question that is not easy to answer. Clearly, globalization costs some Americans their jobs, as it costs millions of workers in other nations their jobs. The textile industry in the Carolinas has been largely smothered by competition from South Asia and elsewhere. But poultry and pork from the American Midwest and South put local farmers around the world out of business. U.S. insurance companies, consulting groups, law firms, advertising agencies, and rock musicians can overwhelm local competition. Let's return to those call centers in Bangalore. If they were in Bangor, Maine, Americans would have those jobs. On the other hand, if the Indian office workers could not afford to dine on tofu made from Brazilian soybeans gathered by Caterpillar

harvesters, some workers in Illinois or elsewhere in the U.S. might get pink slips. A world view of globalization—detached from individual complaints by some companies or labor organizations or others—would acknowledge that globalization makes the world richer. Because of globalization there is simply more stuff to eat, wear, drive around in, and more movies to watch, more books to learn from, more banks to borrow from. So the pile of stuff gets ever bigger, which is good. The vast majority of the world's citizens are better off because of trade. But a sizeable minority, who have lost jobs that are not easily replaced, are worse off. The hard part of globalization is distributing fairly among the world's seven billion people the huge pile of stuff and all the jobs required to produce it.

Q

How does trade affect inflation?

A

It holds inflation down. Rivalry with Japanese and other foreign manufacturers has forced U.S. carmakers to keep their prices in check. Clothing is cheaper in the U.S. because of intense competition among foreign manufacturers. At the same time, beef and poultry and grain raised by superefficient U.S. farmers have helped keep down food prices around the world. This is a large part of what trade is all about, getting better goods and services to more people at cheaper prices. In effect, everybody's income rises. That doesn't explain trade entirely. Sometimes Americans import things because there is no domestic equivalent, such as bananas or the Bolshoi Ballet. And sometimes we import fancy items because of their cachet. An economist friend of ours puzzled over whether to serve at his birthday party expensive Moët champagne, imported from France, or a cheaper sparkling American wine that he knew to be every bit as good. He finally opted for the Moët, fearing his friends would think he had skimped on them if he served the domestic substitute.

Q

What is the balance of trade?

That compares a country's exports to its imports. If a country's imports in a particular time period are worth more than its exports, the country is running a trade deficit. If the exports are worth more, the country is running a trade surplus.

Must a country be in balance with every trading partner?

No. The crucial issue is whether a country's overall exports and imports around the world are in balance. As it happens, the U.S.'s biggest trading partner, Canada, buys almost as much from the U.S. as it sells to the U.S. That eliminates a lot of screaming on both sides of the border. But the U.S.'s second largest partner, China, is a different case. The U.S. sells a lot of high-end electrical equipment, turbines, and aircraft to China each year, but it buys from China three or four times as much in other electrical and power equipment and those familiar toys, games, rugs, crockery, sweatshirts, floor lamps, and on and on. Again, it's not crucial that the U.S. have an almost even trade balance with China, as it does with Canada. And if China were a tiny partner, the 3 or 4 to 1 ratio in China's favor wouldn't matter much. But imports from China are so enormous that even though the U.S. typically runs trade surpluses with Australia, Brazil, the Netherlands, the UK, Turkey, and some others, the surpluses are not enough to offset the huge deficit with China. The U.S. runs more modest deficits with other nations as well and on balance has a trade deficit with the world.

Q&A

Q

What happens when a country runs a trade deficit?

The U.S. economy is so big and complicated that it is difficult to consider balance of trade apart from balance of payments, which we'll get to later on. In the meantime, let's start with a country with a simpler economy, at least as far as international commerce is concerned. When a country like that continues to run a trade deficit, the value of its currency generally declines. Foreigners will not want to hold Ivory Coast francs, say, if foreigners don't need those francs to buy cocoa. Imagine that it takes $1 to exchange for 10 francs to buy a pound of cocoa in the Ivory Coast.

The world perceives that price as too high. Foreigners, therefore, don't want to hold francs because foreigners don't need them to buy cocoa. So there are too many francs in the world—supply exceeds demand; as a result, the value of the franc relative to other currencies will fall. When it takes only 50 cents to buy 10 francs (that is, the value of the franc has dropped by half), the world will start buying Ivory Coast cocoa again. Over time, the fall in the value of the franc increases Ivory Coast exports and thereby reduces the country's trade deficit.

Q

What is the balance of payments?

A

That's a broader category than balance of trade and goes well beyond exports and imports. It includes the balance of trade, but it also includes all the transactions between a country and the rest of the world. It includes all of the investments that people and businesses in one country make in other countries. All the bank accounts people open and stocks and bonds people buy in other countries are figured in as well. The U.S. has a deficit in its balance of trade, as we mentioned earlier. The U.S. buys more oil, cars, food, clothing, furniture, games, and so forth than it sells the world airplanes, computer software, food, medical equipment, movies, and such. So money used for trade flows out of the U.S. That is the trade deficit. But we have a lot of money flowing into the U.S. through our financial and capital accounts. That is, people abroad send more dollars here to buy corporate stocks and bonds and government bonds than we send overseas to buy foreign stocks and bonds. The U.S. is seen as a safe place to put your savings. That is a difference between the U.S. and the Ivory Coast, or for that matter, just about any other nation. To buy those stocks and bonds, foreigners have to change their pesos, pounds, rupees, bhats, or whatever into dollars; that demand for dollars increases the dollar's value relative to other currencies. Also, when interest rates in the U.S. rise, more people want to lend even more dollars to U.S. borrowers because the premiums they pay will be bigger. As a result, the value of the dollar goes up again. Conversely, the value of the dollar goes down when interest rates go down. So for the U.S., the value of its currency is not strictly a matter of trade.

Q

Is it bad for a country when its currency is cheap?

A

Not necessarily. It certainly sounds awful to American ears when we are told that the dollar has dropped in value relative to the euro, say. ("We're not number one anymore?") For that reason no candidate for the U.S. presidency would campaign on a platform of "I will make the dollar cheaper." But the truth is that a fall in the dollar is bad for some Americans, but good for others. When the dollar is low compared to the euro, it is bad for an American buying a Mercedes Benz made in Germany. It takes more dollars to exchange for the euros to buy the German car. Similarly, it becomes more expensive for the American tourist trying to buy a good time in Paris or Venice. However, a weak dollar is good for U.S. exporters and their employees. Industrial machinery and medical devices are big U.S. exports. So when the value of the dollar falls, it becomes cheaper for foreigners to buy U.S.-made power generators and pacemakers, because it takes fewer euros or pesos or whatever to buy the dollars to buy the machinery. Also, when the dollar is cheap, European vacationers crowd into Florida to play on the beaches, and European shoppers flock to New York and San Francisco for bargains.

Q

Do countries manipulate their currencies to keep them cheap?

A

That's what the U.S. accuses the Chinese of doing with the yuan, which is also referred to as the renminbi. China is focused on growth, keeping its products inexpensive in world markets and thereby keeping its manufacturing juggernaut moving full speed ahead. (China isn't much concerned with how much its tourists will have to pay in New York restaurants.) So it doesn't want the yuan to become strong compared to the dollar. How does it keep the yuan cheap? It's a bit complicated. The U.S. dollars flowing into China to buy all those Chinese goods first have to be converted to yuan. By the supply and demand formula, that demand for yuan should push up the yuan's value and lower the value of the dollar. But it doesn't, because the Chinese government uses its dollars to buy things like U.S. Treasury bonds—creating a demand for dollars! The net effect is to keep the yuan from rising in value relative to the dollar. The U.S. complains that because the yuan is artificially cheap, Chinese products are unfairly less expensive than American products that compete with them. At the same time, a weak yuan makes American products more expensive for Chinese to buy and so reduces the amount of exports from the U.S. to China.

Q

What does the World Trade Organization do?

A

The WTO, which has more than 150 member nations representing almost all world trade, is dedicated to making trade as free as possible from tariffs and quotas and other barriers. Since the end of World War II the WTO and its predecessor organization (GATT) have made remarkable progress in freeing the world from protectionist policies by which nations tried to keep outsiders from invading their turf with better, cheaper lawnmowers, overcoats, TV programs, and

telephone service than their native manufacturers, technicians, and others could provide. There are plenty of remaining issues, however. For example, to protect its mom and pop stores, India will not allow big foreign superstores like Walmart into the country. The U.S. continues to subsidize domestic sugar and peanut producers, thus depriving Third World farmers of a big opportunity.

Q&A

Q

What's the World Bank?

A

The bank was set up at the end of World War II to make loans and grants to developing countries for major projects, such as hydroelectric dams, highways, and airports. The money does not go only to big engineering programs. Some of it is spent on education and health programs as well as agriculture and private business development and environmental management. Most of the loans and grants come from the governments of the U.S., Europe, and Japan.

Q

What's the International Monetary Fund?

A

The IMF was created at the same time as the World Bank, and its primary goal is to encourage economic growth and international trade. Unlike the World Bank, the IMF doesn't lend for physical projects like dams. A country that asks for an IMF loan is struggling through a financial crisis, or wildly fluctuating trade levels, or falling or rising exchange rates. Recipients are often so debt ridden that they can't borrow from private lenders to pay their expenses, such as salaries for schoolteachers and police. Early on, most of the nations that received IMF aid were in the Third World. But more recently when Greece, Ireland, and Portugal got head over heels in debt, the IMF stepped in to help as well. Again, the loans come mostly from the major industrial nations. As a condition for getting a loan, the receiving country has to work toward getting its finances in order, generally by cutting government expenses and reforming tax policies and practices.

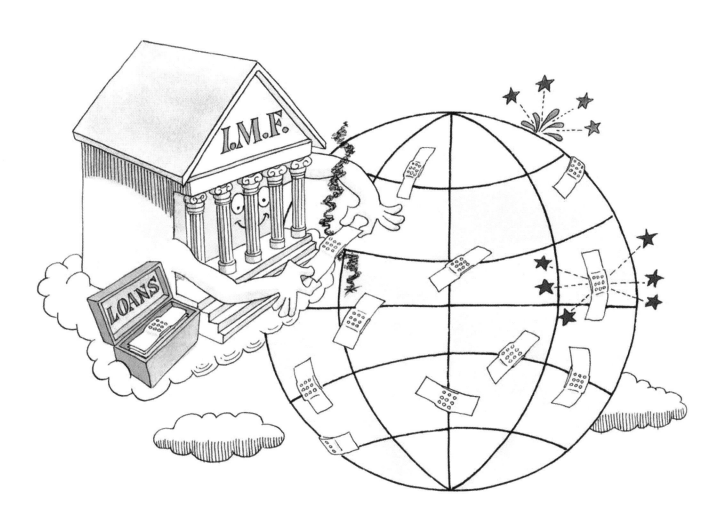

Q

What is the G-20?

It's a gathering of the 20 nations with the world's largest economies, representing about 80% of gross world product and 85% of world trade. Finance ministers, treasury secretaries, central bank governors, and sometimes presidents and prime ministers meet periodically and attempt to coordinate economic policies so that they are all working together rather than against one another. (Sometimes only eight of the members meet—these are the G-8.) The attempt is not always successful. In 2008, for example, as the world economy slumped following the global financial/housing crisis, the U.S. urged Germany to stimulate its economy to increase the total of world demand. Germany declined, fearing that a stimulus might lead to inflation. From the perspective of the Germans and some others, the focus should have been on reducing government debt. For the Americans, the key concern was getting world economies churning again.

What is the World Economic Forum?

It's a Swiss, non-profit foundation that brings together every winter in Davos, Switzerland, many of the world's top business and political leaders, intellectuals, and journalists to discuss the most pressing issues facing the world, not just economic issues, but health, environmental, and political ones as well. The Forum does not have any direct power, that is, it doesn't distribute money to needy recipients or make political decisions. But the very influential people who gather in Davos get to swap ideas. The media pay attention.

RIPPLES AND WAVES

What happens next? How to anticipate the possible consequences of economic events

Events beget other events, like a rock tossed into a pond. On the waters of economics, however, ripples can turn into mighty waves, sometimes lifting the fortunes of people and nations to new and prosperous heights and sometimes plunging them to despairing depths.

When a debt crisis struck Europe in the summer of 2011, a wave soon stormed ashore in the U.S., drenching surprised American investors and washing billions of dollars out of their collective portfolios. Many of those investors had no idea they were so close to Europe. What happened?

U.S. investment banks had bought millions of dollars worth of Greek and Italian government bonds. So when the values of the bonds nose-dived because of doubts those governments could pay their debts, the stocks of U.S. investment banks suffered. Also, European investment banks own, among their assets, Greek and Italian government bonds as well as stock in U.S. companies. When the value of the bonds plummets, they can cover some of their losses by selling U.S. stocks, flooding the market and so pushing down the value of those U.S. stocks.

Moreover, the European Union and the UK are huge customers for U.S. products, accounting for almost 20% of all U.S. exports—everything from chemicals, pharmaceuticals, machine tools, and planes to consulting firm services, computer software, and movies. Companies like Ford, GM, Dow Chemical, DuPont, IBM, and GE have enormous operations and sales overseas. When Europeans tighten their belts because of recession, or just fear of recession, U.S. exporters will be battered. So investors sell off big name stocks and those of the hundreds of smaller U.S. companies that are suppliers to the Fords and GEs. The upside of this U.S. dependence on Europe is, of course, that when Europe prospers, the consequences are better living for lots of American workers and stockholders.

What are the effects of other major events, comparable to the European debt crisis, and what are the consequences of actions taken by government to push or pull the U.S. economy in one direction or another? On the following pages we look at 10 of them and try to track how they *might* reverberate through the economy. *Might* is an important qualifier here. The wisest forecaster can be embarrassed by the random forces at work throughout the economic world; sometimes those forces magnify the expected results in a sequence, and sometimes they diminish them or knock them off course altogether. Disruptions can be huge and come out of nowhere. Who would have predicted that a tsunami striking the coast of Japan would break supply chains leading to U.S. auto factories and change the way the world thinks about nuclear energy?

Cautiously, we pose what is likely to happen if:

The dollar gets weaker

- Trips to Europe get more expensive and Americans spend more on vacations closer to home in the U.S.
- Imported BMWs are too pricey, and Americans buy domestically made cars
- French shoppers flock to New York stores for bargains
- German tourists crowd Miami beaches and hotels
- English movie lovers buy more Hollywood DVDs
- Australians buy more medications from the U.S.

The dollar gets stronger

- Chinese home furnishings and toys are cheaper
- Japanese have to pay more for U.S. planes and soybeans
- Americans ignore the Jersey shore and summer in Spain
- U.S. manufacturers buy less expensive parts in Europe, so their final products are cheaper
- Washington hotels and restaurants suffer as Canadian tourists stay home

Interest rates rise

- Homeowners can't afford to pay for large mortgages; housing prices rise more slowly, or even drop; and buyers purchase smaller homes
- Entrepreneurs can't afford loans to start businesses, and employment falters
- Foreigners buy U.S. Treasury bonds because higher interest rates mean that returns are bigger and more attractive than alternative investments
- Foreigners' need for dollars to buy Treasuries makes the dollar stronger
- Rising cost of the dollar makes U.S. goods more expensive overseas
- Exports decline

The stock market falls

- Investors, especially retirees, get nervous and curtail their spending
- Economy weakens as consumers buy less
- New companies delay IPOs because investors are cautious
- Investors take money out of the stock market and invest in housing, speculating that home prices will rise
- Universities raise tuitions as values of their endowments decline
- Optimistic young workers buy stocks cheap
- Small ripples: Some investors shift savings to gold, lifting price of gold; families search drawers for forgotten watches, other gold jewelry

The government cuts spending on goods and services

- Some large businesses lose their best customer
- Some government workers lose their jobs
- A naval shipyard reduces shifts, and restaurants and other small businesses in the neighborhood collapse
- Employments declines steeply in some regions
- GDP shrinks

The government reduces individual income taxes

- Taxpayers have more cash and, if they feel confident about the economy, spend on consumer goods across the board
- Businesses enjoy record-setting sales
- Employment rises as new businesses start
- Inflation rises as well and causes concern
- Deficit increases because of lower tax revenues

The government reduces business taxes

- U.S. businesses that had moved operations overseas for lower taxes bring them back to the U.S.
- Established businesses record more after-tax profits and may expand
- Entrepreneurs open new businesses
- Employment goes up and the economy grows
- Inflation creeps upward and deficits start to rise

The Federal Reserve buys U.S. government bonds from banks

- In exchange for bonds, banks take money from the Fed; the money supply increases
- Bank deposits and reserves go up
- Interest rates fall because there is more money around, that is, the supply of money is increasing faster than demand
- Loans are easier to get for both businesses and consumers
- Consumers and businesses borrow, invest, and spend
- The economy grows

The Federal Reserve sells U.S. government bonds to banks

- Banks pay for the bonds with their deposits and reserves
- The money supply decreases as a result
- With fewer reserves, banks have to cut back on the loans they issue
- Interest rates rise
- There is less money for businesses to expand their enterprises and for consumers to buy homes and cars
- The economy shrinks

The government increases spending or cuts taxes without surpluses to cover a shortfall

- Government has to borrow more
- Government need for loans drives up interest rates
- Businesses can't afford those higher rates and are crowded out
- Business investment and expansion decline
- Economic growth slows and so does the rise in individual and business incomes

KEY WORDS AND PHRASES

A glossary to help you understand a complex economic world

Alternative minimum tax

Designed to limit the amount of deductions for mortgages, charitable giving, state and local taxes, and such, that very high income earners can claim on their federal tax returns.

Automatic stabilizers

Aspects of the federal budget that automatically offset expansions and contractions. For example, people pay more taxes during an expansion, which reduces the amount of income they have to spend elsewhere. Conversely, they pay fewer taxes when the economy sputters.

Bailout

Government payout to keep a business from failing. The rationale is that the collapse of a big bank or automaker, for example, would create a lot of pain beyond the particular business being rescued.

Balance of payments

The combination of the balance of trade plus the balance on the financial and capital accounts (see page 220).

Balance of trade

A nation's exports minus its imports (see page 214).

Balanced Budget Amendment

This proposed Constitutional amendment would forbid the federal government from running a deficit in any year (see page 106).

Bank failure

A bank often fails when its assets—that is, the money it has lent to people—aren't generating enough income to pay the bank's depositors. For nonbankers it's always a little hard to get one's head around this, but a bank's assets are not money in its vaults; it is the money the bank has out on the street. That's what produces income.

Bank run

A story, true or false, spreads that a bank is failing, perhaps because of bad loans. Depositors rush to get their money, and because banks never, or rarely, have the cash on hand to meet that kind of demand, the bank closes, maybe permanently. Rushing to the bank is not necessary for Americans these days because the FDIC (see page 243) insures their deposits for up to $250,000 per depositor.

Bankruptcy

When you hear that a company is bankrupt, that is, can't pay its bills, you might think it is going out of business; not necessarily. True, a Chapter 7 bankruptcy generally means a company is being liquidated or sold to someone else. But a Chapter 11 bankruptcy allows a company to reorganize and keep operating as it bargains with its creditors. General Motors is a recent, striking example of Chapter 11.

Barter

The oldest form of trade (see pages 12–17).

Bonds

Corporations and governments borrow money by selling pieces of paper specifying that each year they will pay the holder of the bond a fixed dollar amount of money. The market value of the bond you own will go up and down over time. Let's say you paid $1,000 for a bond that pays $50 a year, which works out to a simple 5%. Suppose interest rates in general rise, and some other companies or governments of equal standing then issue $500 bonds that also pay $50, or 10%. They have to do that to attract investors. So your $1,000 bond isn't really worth $1,000 on the market; based on what it pays you or anyone you sell it to, it's worth $500, the same as that recently issued $500 bond. The good news is that the value of your bond can go up in the same way.

Bond yields

You have to think upside down when you read about bond yields in the newspaper. When stock prices go up, that generally means the economy is doing well and so are you, shareholder. That's clear enough. But when bond yields go up, that means the value of your bonds is actually going down. Here's the reason. The yield refers to the percent interest the bond pays. When the bond that pays $50 a year is valued at $1,000, it is paying a yield of 5%. When the bond's value drops to $500, its yield jumps to 10%, because $50 is 10% of $500.

Bubbles
Prices of an asset or assets swell so large that wise people scratch their heads because the high prices make no sense. If it's a bubble, in time it will burst (see page 200).

Business cycle
The ups and downs of the economy. A decrease in spending and employment followed by recovery, with the economy reaching a high level of employment, production, and income, generally higher than the previous peak.

CAC 40
An index of stock prices of the 40 most significant large companies on the French stock market.

Call
The right to buy, or call, a share of stock from someone else at some time in the future at a specified price.

Capacity
How much an industry, or the economy in general, can produce. If the copper industry has enough mines, factories, workers, and managers to turn out twice as much copper wire as it currently does, the industry is operating at 50% of capacity.

Capital
It has a couple of quite different meanings. For banks and other financial institutions, capital is all the money, stocks, and other holdings the bank's shareholders have invested in the bank plus all the profits earned, minus the dividends paid to shareholders and any losses. When economists use the word capital they often mean one of the factors of production, along with labor, management, and resources. This kind of capital, sometimes called physical capital, is not money, but rather machinery and factories and such.

Capital gain
When you sell an asset, which can be a stock, a house, or just about anything else, the difference between the price you paid for it and the bigger price you sold it for is a capital gain. If you sell it for less, that's a capital loss. A capital gain is often taxed at a lower rate than ordinary income.

Central bank
A government or quasi-government institution—like the Federal Reserve in the U.S.—that is charged with managing a country's money supply.

Collateralized debt obligation (CDO)
The highfalutin name itself should arouse suspicion. A debt is an obligation by definition, so why the redundancy? Think of these things as bonds backed up by collateral; the collateral can be many things, including a bunch of home mortgages. Some of those mortgages are good, that is, the homeowners make their monthly mortgage payments. But so many went bad in the first decade of the 2000s that CDOs were a major factor in the housing collapse and recession that followed.

Commercial bank
A bank that takes deposits and makes loans.

Consumption
Spending by individuals on goods and services.

Consumption tax
Similar to a sales tax; some see it as a potential substitute for the income tax (see page 78).

Credit default swap
A kind of insurance policy that protects the buyer of a security (see page 198).

Currency
A nation's medium of exchange, including its bills and coins, such as dollars, euros, and yen.

Currency manipulation
A country buys and sells its currency and the currencies of other counties to control the value of its own currency.

Cyclical deficit
The part of the federal deficit that is caused by falling tax receipts and rising spending on transfer payments, such as unemployment insurance, during an economic slowdown.

Deflation
Prices fall for a period lasting at least a couple of months; the opposite of inflation.

Derivatives
A financial instrument (clumsy term which refers to the universe of holdings that include stocks, bonds, and so forth) whose value is dependent on (or derived from) another financial instrument. Traditional derivatives include futures that help farmers guarantee prices for crops now in the ground and help airlines guarantee future fuel prices. Some other derivatives helped cause the financial crisis of 2007–2009 (see pages 196–199).

Discount rate
Banks can borrow from the Federal Reserve at what is called the discount rate when other banks won't lend to them. That can happen because the borrowing bank is at risk, or simply because interest rates that it must pay those other banks are discouragingly high.

Discount window
The place where banks borrow at the discount rate. In a simpler time there was an actual window by that name in the Federal Reserve Banks.

Discretionary spending
The government spending that has been decided upon through the usual tug of war among the houses of Congress and the White House. It is distinct from entitlements and other mandatory spending.

Dodd–Frank Reform Act
Named for a senator and congressman, this 2010 legislation would do a lot of things, among them create a watchdog agency to make sure consumers understand their banks' practices. It would also require that banks be backed up by enough capital so they don't have to be rescued by taxpayers during crises.

Dow Jones Industrial Average
A number that daily tracks the stock prices of 30 leading U.S. companies and is a shorthand reading of whether Wall Street's day has been good or bad. When people ask "How did the Market do today?" they are generally inquiring about the fate of the "Dow" and a couple of other indexes, like the NASDAQ and the Standard & Poor's 500.

Economic growth
A real expansion, as distinct from nominal (inflation-caused) expansion, in gross domestic product.

Electronic money
Deposits in bank accounts that can be transferred to someone else electronically through an EFT (electronic funds transfer).

Emerging markets
Fast-developing countries that are favorite places for adventurous investors to send their money. The countries include some big, presumably stable economies like those of Brazil, China, and India, but also riskier ones like Egypt and Thailand.

Entitlements
Social Security, Medicare, Medicaid, and other services that people are automatically entitled to because they have reached a certain age or have low incomes.

Equity
Ownership. The part of a house that you own, as distinct from what you owe the bank, is your equity. Stocks are sometimes called equities, because they represent a stockholder's ownership of the company. Bonds, as distinct from equity, represent money the bondholder has lent to the company.

ETF (exchange traded fund)
A collection of stocks, bonds, or commodities that can be traded on exchanges during the day much the way individual stocks are traded. They are different from mutual funds, which are priced only at the end of the day.

Exchange rates
The rate of exchange of one currency for another, for example 12 pesos for a dollar.

Excise taxes
Taxes placed on particular goods and services, such as alcohol, cigarettes, and gasoline.

Fannie Mae (Federal National Mortgage Association)
Fannie Mae buys mortgages from banks and other lenders, putting money into the hands of those lenders so they can originate even more mortgages. Although it was originally sponsored by the government to promote home ownership, Fannie Mae became a publicly traded company; in 2008, it was taken over by the federal government as part of the efforts to calm financial markets.

FDIC (Federal Deposit Insurance Corporation)
An event that used to exacerbate a financial crisis was the bank run. Depositors would get panicky and rush to withdraw all their money from their banks. Banks almost never have enough cash on hand to satisfy those demands. In 1933 the FDIC was created, guaranteeing depositors that no matter what happens to the bank, each depositor's account will be reimbursed, these days for up to $250,000.

Fed funds rate
The interest rate that banks charge one another for loans. The Federal Reserve keeps a close eye on this rate because the rate has a big impact on interest rates in general (see page 164).

Federal debt
The accumulation of all of the federal government's past deficits and surpluses (see page 94).

Federal debt limit
A law that sets a maximum level for the federal debt. Once the limit is reached, Congress and the President have to raise it, or cut spending and/or increase taxes.

Federal deficit/surplus
When spending is greater than revenues in a given year, the federal government is running a deficit. If revenues are bigger than spending, it's called a surplus (see page 94).

Federal Reserve System
The U.S. central bank, aka the Fed, acts independently of both Congress and the President, but its seven governors are nominated by the President and approved by the Senate. Also, the Fed has to keep Congress informed of what it is doing. The Fed has 12 district banks around the country. Each provides services to local banks, such as distributing currency; they also supervise local banks (see Chapter 5).

Federal Trade Commission (FTC)
It has a number of missions, very important among them guarding against monopolies and other restraints of trade. Its jurisdiction often overlaps that of the Justice Department's antitrust division.

Fiat money
Money because the government says it's money with no promise of gold, silver, or other valuables to back it up.

Financial and capital account
The flows of money into and out of a nation for investments.

Financial instrument
No, not a valuable Stradivarius, but a stock, bond, put, call, swap, option, or similar tool of finance.

Fiscal policy
The use of taxing and spending to encourage or discourage economic activity (see page 68).

Fitch Ratings
A private agency that rates the creditworthiness of corporate and government bonds. Two other agencies, Moody's and Standard & Poor's, perform the same service.

Flat tax
An income tax that is a fixed percentage on all incomes (see page 76).

FOMC (Federal Open Market Committee)
The governors of the Federal Reserve, plus the presidents of five Fed banks, who meet about eight times a year (see pages 128, 132, and **Open market operations**).

Foreign direct investment
Individuals or companies can buy and take control or share in control of foreign companies. It is distinct from portfolio investment, which refers to owning shares in a company without participating in its management.

Forwards
Another name for contracts to buy or sell an asset, typically a commodity, for a set price in the future. Unlike futures, forwards are private agreements and are not traded on an exchange.

Freddie Mac (Federal Home Loan Mortgage Corporation)
Like Fannie Mae, it buys mortgages from banks and other lenders. It then packages the mortgages and sells them to investors as mortgage-backed securities. That puts more money into Freddie Mac's hands to buy more mortgages. It was a publicly traded company, but was taken over by the federal government in 2008 as part of the efforts to calm financial markets.

FTSE 100
"Footsie" is an index of 100 stocks of large companies traded on the London Stock Exchange.

Futures
Not surprisingly, futures are contracts to buy and sell bonds, stocks, currencies, other financial instruments, commodities, and agriculture products in the future. They are agreements to buy and sell a given amount at a set price on a specified date. Futures are similar to forwards, but they are standardized and are traded on exchanges like the Chicago Mercantile Exchange.

G-20 and G-8
The bigger group is made up of the world's 20 largest economies, which get together to talk about common economic concerns; the smaller group (all of whose members are in the G-20) talk about issues beyond economics, such as health, law enforcement, energy, and the environment.

GDP (Gross Domestic Product)
The value of a nation's output, measured in dollars or another currency (see page 46).

Glass-Steagall Act
Named for a senator and a congressman, this 1933 act created the Federal Deposit Insurance Corporation and, more controversially, separated investment banks from commercial banks to prevent conflict of interest hanky-panky. For example, the commercial side of the bank might recklessly lend a lot of depositors' money to a wobbly client of the investment side.

Globalization
The interconnection of the world's economies (see pages 203–204).

Gold standard
The linkage of a currency to gold. Until 1971 the U.S. government would give foreign governments an ounce of gold for $35. Some theorists want to return the U.S. to the gold standard, but most economists fear that would severely limit the effectiveness of monetary policy.

Goldilocks economy
Not too hot, not too cold. Economists think a growth rate of about 3% or 4% year is just right for the U.S.

Haircut
When the value of the loan you made is shaved down because the borrower can't pay it all back.

Hedge funds
Pools of money that wealthy investors place in ventures, often riskier than mutual funds, such as oil and gas exploration or complex commodity trading, that others overlook or bypass. Hedge fund managers use complicated mixes of investment strategies to enhance return and manage risk (see page 192).

House Ways & Means Committee
The U.S. Constitution says tax bills begin here.

Index
An average of the prices of stocks or bonds, used by investors and economists to measure the increase (or decrease) in value. If the S&P 500 increases by 7% one year, it means that, on average, prices of stocks included in the index increased by 7%.

Inflation
When prices rise for at least a couple of months; the opposite of deflation.

Initial Public Offering (IPO)
When a private company goes public (see page 182).

Interest on reserves
Recent legislation allows the Fed to pay banks interest on the amount they hold in reserve. That's a very powerful new tool that would discourage banks from lending in an overheating economy and thereby help cool it.

International Monetary Fund (IMF)
It provides financial assistance to countries in trouble; it is usually headed by a European (see page 230).

Investment bank
A company or partnership that advises big corporations on their best financial moves. These banks also make a lot of money trading stocks and bonds. Goldman Sachs and Morgan Stanley are among the largest (see page 180).

Junk bonds
A rare instance on Wall Street in which the name actually understates the value. They aren't really junk; they're just riskier than top-rated bonds and as a result have to pay higher interest to attract buyers.

Keynesians
Economists who in the tradition of John Maynard Keynes emphasize the importance of changes in spending as the primary factor in changing economic conditions. Among their rivals are the Monetarists (see below).

Leverage
Borrowing in order to magnify the rate of return on an investment (see page 188).

LIBOR (London Interbank Offered Rate)
You don't have to remember what the initials stand for. It's the interest rate British banks charge one another to borrow money for up to a year, and is generally the cheapest interest rate on the planet. Changes in LIBOR can be a signal of where interest rates in general are headed.

Mandatory spending
It includes entitlements and also such required outlays as interest on the federal debt.

Mercantile exchanges
The two big ones, in New York and Chicago, serve as places for buying and selling futures and other financial instruments based on the prices of commodities, such as sugar, oats, cotton, pigs.

Monetarists
Economists who emphasize the importance of changes in the money supply as the primary factor in determining economic conditions. Among their rivals are the Keynesians (see above).

Monetary policy
The use of changes in the money supply to influence the economy (see page 122).

Money supply
Generally, the total amount of currency in circulation, plus the much bigger pile of deposits in a wide variety of bank accounts and money market mutual funds.

Moody's
A private agency that rates the creditworthiness of companies and governments that issue bonds. Two other agencies, Standard & Poor's and Fitch Ratings, perform the same service.

Moral hazard
This peculiar term refers to the way people behave when they think someone else will pay for their losses. In other words, a big bank might take huge risks because if worse comes to worst, the government will bail it out.

Mortgage
Generally a loan secured by real property, such as a house or office building. The strange word seems to come from the French for "dead pledge." What that means is not clear.

Mortgage-backed securities
Securities that consist of a bunch of mortgages, especially home mortgages.

Multiplier effect
There are two of them. The *spending* multiplier comes about when income moves through the economy because consumers are spending it, and that produces even more spending (see page 82). Economists sometimes argue that when trying to boost an economy it's more effective to give money to the poor than to the rich: The poor will spend it quickly; the rich might save it. The *money* multiplier occurs when the Federal Reserve buys bonds and creates new money (see pages 140–153).

Mutual fund
A pool of stocks or bonds, an investment distinct from owning individual stocks or bonds. Financial advisers often suggest these pools as safer than buying stocks in a few individual companies.

NASDAQ
A stock exchange made up mostly of companies smaller than those traded on the New York Stock Exchange. It also has a significant component of high-tech stocks. The NASDAQ Composite Index, known as the NASDAQ, is an index of the prices of all the stocks listed on this exchange. Like the Dow, its day-to-day price fluctuation is an indicator of how stocks in general are moving.

New York Stock Exchange
The world's largest stock exchange, as measured by the total market value of all 4,000 or so company stocks that are traded on it.

NIKKEI Index
An index of 225 large company stocks traded on the Tokyo Stock Exchange.

Open market operations
The Federal Reserve sells and buys bonds to and from a handful of large private dealers to influence the money supply and interest rates.

Options
The right to buy or sell shares of stock at a set price during a particular time period. Puts and calls are types of options. Also, it's common practice for companies to pay their executives partly with stock options. Let's imagine that you go to work for Big Wheels and are given options to buy 1,000 shares of Big Wheels for $60 a share anytime during the next two years. If BW is now trading at $50 a share, your options are underwater (worthless) for the time being. But if BW's price rises to $100 a share, you can buy 1,000 from the company for $60 a share, sell them for $100, and pocket $40 a share.

Payroll taxes
Social Security and Medicare taxes.

Prime rate
The interest rate that banks and other lenders charge their best and most reliable customers.

Private equity funds
Pools of money that wealthy investors use to buy troubled companies, rehab them, and then resell them (see page 194).

Productivity
The output that each worker produces, a key to raising living standards (see page 54).

Put
The right to sell (or put) a share of stock to someone at a set price for a specified time.

Quantitative easing
The Federal Reserve doesn't employ poets, so you get this clumsy phrase to explain the following: When interest rates are already about as low as they can go, the Fed may continue to expand the money supply to make bank lending even easier. The ultimate goal is to stimulate spending and employment (see Chapter 5).

Quants
Conventional securities analysts evaluate an asset, a stock issued by a company, say, by a number of measures, everything from the company's market share to the quality of its management. Quantitative analysts, or "quants" as they became known in their breathtaking rise to influence, rely exclusively on numbers, complicated algorithms that only a few understand.

Quotas
A limit on the amount or value of imports in order to protect domestic producers from competition.

Recession
A significant decline in activity across the entire economy that lasts for more than a few months.

Reserve requirements
The percentage of deposits that banks are required to keep in reserve, that is, not lend.

S&P 500
An index of the stock prices of 500 major U.S. companies compiled by Standard & Poor's, similar to the Dow Jones Industrial Average.

Securities
Usually stocks (equities), but can sometimes refer to bonds and other financial instruments that can be easily bought and sold.

Securities analyst
He or she evaluates corporations to advise investors on whether to buy their stocks.

Securities and Exchange Commission (SEC)
Founded in 1934 during the Great Depression, the SEC polices stock and options exchanges and tries to keep corporations and others from deceiving investors. The SEC has had success in detecting insider trading, but it failed to uncover Bernard Madoff's biggest Ponzi scheme ever.

Securitization
Taking a bunch of existing loans or other kinds of debt and gathering them into a new financial instrument, such as mortgage-backed securities.

Senate Finance Committee
The Senate committee responsible for examining the House of Representatives' proposed tax legislation and drafting its own.

SENSEX
An index of 30 major Indian stocks traded on the Bombay (Mumbai) Stock Exchange.

Short sale
Borrowing shares of stock from someone and selling them, with the promise to return an equal number of shares to the original owner later on. People who do this ("shorts") hope to replace the shares they borrowed with new shares they bought more cheaply (see page 190).

Sovereign wealth fund
An investment fund, which can include stocks, bonds, commodities, and other assets, owned by a government. China, Russia, and Persian Gulf states are among those that control huge funds with significant economic clout. Less authoritarian states, such as Canada and Norway, also have such funds.

Stagflation
Theoretically, there's a trade-off that causes inflation to drop when an economy slows down. It doesn't always work that smoothly, so it's possible to have an economy stumble at a halting pace while inflation remains high. The most common cause is rapidly rising energy prices.

Standard and Poor's
A private agency (part of McGraw-Hill) that rates corporate stocks and bonds and government bonds.

Stimulus
Government action, either fiscal or monetary, to energize the economy when it is faltering (see pages 82–85).

Stocks
Shares of ownership in a company; also called equities.

STOXX Europe 600
An index of 600 small, medium, and large European company stocks.

Structural deficit
The federal deficit that would exist at full employment (economists consider we're at full employment when about 95% of the work force is employed). The actual deficit is higher when unemployment is high, because the unemployed are not paying taxes and contributing to federal revenues.

Subprime mortgages
Mortgages to people who don't have the credit and employment records to qualify for traditional home mortgages. Because subprime mortgages are considered risky, their interest rates are generally higher.

Supply-side economics

A concept popularized during the Reagan administration. Part of its theory was that if tax rates were sharply reduced, business owners would start new businesses and workers would work harder because they got to keep more of their earnings. The supply of goods and services would increase, and even though tax rates were lower, the increased economic activity would actually increase tax revenues. Although this is theoretically possible, in the real world there are no examples of total income tax receipts increasing as a result of tax rate cuts.

Swaps

A swap is a kind of insurance policy, a hedge against something going wrong. One investor "swaps," or trades, the revenues or obligations of one financial instrument for those of another. A notorious example is the credit default swap (see page 241), which played a significant role in the financial crisis of 2007–2009. Often to protect themselves from swings in interest rates, individuals and firms swap a fixed interest rate on a loan for a variable interest rate on a similar loan; to protect themselves from swings in exchange rates, firms or individuals exchange a financial instrument in one currency for a similar instrument in a different currency.

Tariffs

Taxes placed on imported goods. Like quotas, they are designed to discourage imports and protect domestic producers.

TARP (Troubled Asset Relief Program)

A federal government effort started in 2008 to buy from financial institutions their holdings of CDOs (see page 241) and other assets considered so toxic, or at least chancy, that no one else would touch them. The goal was to keep critical financial institutions from collapsing.

Taxes, progressive and regressive

Progressive taxes fall hardest on the wealthy, such as higher percentage rates they pay on income at the top of the income scale. Regressive taxes are across-the-board taxes, such as sales taxes, in which everyone pays the same rate regardless of income. Because a dollar in taxes is more difficult for a poor man than a rich one, a regressive tax falls harder on the poor.

Too big to fail

Companies, banks, and other financial institutions that have grown so big their failure would create disaster well beyond their walls. So the federal government sometimes feels an obligation to save them. The federal government in effect bought General Motors stock because the failure of GM could have pulled down its supplier network and put many thousands out of work. Huge banks and insurance companies are so entwined in buying from and selling to one another that the failure of a big one would create panic throughout the industry.

Toxic assets

Assets that are worthless, or are at least are so uncertain that few will buy them and they are worth significantly less than their initial value. Individual CDOs (see page 241) often contain a mixture of reliable mortgages and hopeless ones, but during the housing bubble neither CDO sellers nor buyers bothered to figure out how many of each kind were in a package. Therefore many CDOs became toxic.

Trade deficit/ surplus

When a country imports more than it exports, it runs a deficit; when it exports more, it runs a surplus.

Transfer payments

Social Security, unemployment and welfare payments, and other support that government gives citizens to boost their income. It does not include support in the form of medical care, such as Medicare and Medicaid.

Treasury Bills, Bonds, Notes, Securities

Also known as Treasuries. They all refer to loans by investors to the U.S. government. The difference among them is generally the time it takes for them to come to maturity; at maturity the government must then pay up the dollar amount stated on the loan.

Unemployment rate

That's pretty obviously the percentage of the labor force out of work. The official rate generally understates the real unemployment rate, however, because it doesn't include people who are so discouraged about their prospects they are no longer looking for work.

Value Added Tax (VAT)

Similar to a consumption tax and a sales tax, but unlike them it's not just a tax on the final product sold at retail. Under VAT, there would be a tax on every step of making and distributing an industrial product, say, a toaster. The maker of the steel for the electric coils would include a tax on what he charged the coil maker; the coil maker would include a tax based on the difference between what he paid the steel maker and what he charged the toaster maker, and so forth. Each step of the way, a tax would be paid to the government. Ultimately, all the tax costs would be borne by the consumer in the retail price of the toaster.

Venture capital

Financing provided to young, promising, high-risk enterprises, especially in high tech. Many VCs, as venture capitalists are known, are located in Silicon Valley, but they get their capital, that is, their money, from rich individuals, university endowments, retirement funds, hedge funds, and others everywhere.

VIX

A type of index that is designed to show investors' expectations of volatility in stocks included in the S&P 500, sometimes called the "fear index."

World Bank

An international institution, mostly financed by large industrial countries, to make loans to developing countries; it is usually headed by an American (see page 228).

World Economic Forum

A non-profit foundation that annually brings together business and political leaders and others from around the world to discuss major global issues (see page 234).

World Trade Organization (WTO)

A group of more than 150 nations dedicated to making trade as free as possible (see page 226).

Yield curve

A graph showing the difference between short-term and longer-term interest rates (see pages 166–173). Short-term bonds generally pay lower interest rates than longer-term bonds because to get investors to tie up their money for a long time, you have to pay them higher interest rates. If there is uncertainty about the future of the economy, that relationship may change, so that short-term bonds are paying higher interest rates. Therefore, a change in the yield curve could be a signal there is trouble ahead.